Contents

Introduction

The period and the events covered by these two units contain a considerably more complicated range of developments than that covered in Units 3–4. Then we were able to concentrate on the Arts and Crafts Movement and Art Nouveau in Britain, Belgium and France as the most important areas of study. The fourteen years which led up to the First World War, however, cannot be categorized so easily. In many ways, the most noticeable development in Europe is a reaction against the Art Nouveau, towards various forms of classicism. This is particularly apparent in Germany and yet this movement towards solid monumentality, expressing as it does the increasing confidence and economic and political power of a united Germany, contains many seeds of the spectacular changes in thought and style which followed the war.

The classicism of this period is not as obviously a revival of earlier stylistic forms as most of the 'Revivals' of the nineteenth century, but more to do with trying to build up a consistent, workable and dignified style suitable not only for big public buildings and factories, but also for individual houses and working-class mass housing. It represents a return to professionalism after the excitement and amateurism of much of the Arts and Crafts and Art Nouveau period. Nevertheless, as we will see, elements of Art Nouveau and of the Arts and Crafts persisted throughout the period.

Running through these pre-war years, and continuing through this century, there is a ground-swell of what we have called the 'vernacular revival', which in many ways can be seen as an attempt to break away from the idea of style at all. Owing a great deal to the British Arts and Crafts architects and writers, German and Austrian architects and designers tried to find again the simple, 'honest' values which characterized the village and country architecture of their homeland. At one extreme, this contained strong regionalist elements which insisted that a building should reflect and embody the materials, character and traditions of the precise area, the 'ground', where it was constructed. According to this school of thought, anything different would destroy the character of the area and stand out like an excrescence, however well designed and excellent in itself. In another form, we find similar ideas in what has been called 'national romanticism', which describes the efforts made by architects all over Europe to revive and capture the truly national and characteristic aesthetic of the country as a whole, using not only local building methods and materials, but also recognizable national styles. We have seen examples of this attitude clearly expressed in the 1900 Exhibition in Paris. Linked with this was an interest in the traditional building 'types': the simple farm house, or the modest terrace row. For this reason, the vernacular tradition did not always run counter to other developments in modern architecture, but, as in the case of Voysey, Mackintosh and, on the whole, Baillie Scott, reinforced it and prepared the way for many later developments. We shall see this particularly in the examples of Heinrich Tessenow and Adolf Loos.

In Part Three, we will investigate the influence of Art Nouveau in Germany and Austria, which was transformed into the German *Jugendstil* and the Austrian *Sezessionstil*. We will also look at the Viennese influence in general, which contained many classical elements due to the teaching of Otto Wagner and his disciples. In Part Four we will look at the various attempts to achieve a new, stripped, classical monumentality in Germany and France. In Part Five we will look at the major effort of German designers and architects to re-align their efforts towards an understanding and mastery of mechanical production and the new possibilities of construction. The efforts of the *Deutscher Werkbund* in particular were to be extremely important for design throughout Europe after the First World War. We will try to see whether there were fundamental changes in outlook and aesthetic, or whether these were only modifications of earlier ideas. A complicated programme, then, and one in which the different themes we have tried to disentangle are all, in some way, interconnected.

AIMS

1 To investigate whether there is a logical development which ties together all the activities of the period.

2 To look for major changes in outlook and formal expression in the period.

3 To trace the impact on architecture and design of the economic and technological developments of the period.

AUTHORS' ACKNOWLEDGEMENTS

Stefan Muthesius, Lecturer, University of East Anglia, wrote most of the material on architecture. Bridget Wilkins, Senior Lecturer, Middlesex Polytechnic, wrote most of the material on design. Tim Benton wrote sections 3 and 4 in Part 6, and linking material elsewhere in the units. The authors wish to acknowledge the helpful comments of the Course Team, and in particular Charlotte Benton, Elizabeth Deighton and Geoffrey Newman.

BROADCAST PROGRAMMES

Television   Industrial Architecture: AEG and Fagus factories

In this programme, Tim Benton compares the industrial buildings by Peter Behrens for the AEG (General Electrical Company of Germany) in Berlin with the almost exactly contemporaneous factory which Walter Gropius designed for Karl Benscheidt's Fagus shoe-last factory, in Alfeld-an-der-Leine. The comparison has a particular point since Gropius was working for Behrens on the earlier AEG buildings, and the Fagus factory was the first building he designed after leaving Behrens's office. Furthermore, the Fagus factory is often referred to as the first really 'modern' building, while the AEG buildings, at first sight, appear to have a markedly classical aesthetic. It is is important that you read the section in Part Six

entitled 'New developments in German Industrial Architecture' before watching this programme.

Radiovision   Tony Garnier: The Cité Industrielle

Dr Dora Wiebenson wrote and presented this programme for us, on a subject which she has researched and written about (see recommended reading). We have had to leave Tony Garnier out of our treatment in these units, because most of his influence came after the war, on the architects of Le Corbusier's generation. His two volume project for a city of the future was important not only for its town planning reforms, but also for his advocacy of the use of reinforced concrete. If you would like to prepare for this programme, read *Banham*, Chapter 3, and *Hitchcock*, Chapter 18.

Radiovision   Reinforced Concrete: Hennebique to Perret

Professor Peter Collins, who has written the standard work on the use of reinforced concrete by men like August Perret (see recommended reading) recorded this programme for us. Hennebique and Perret mastered the intractable problems of reinforced concrete and Perret evolved a mature, but restrained language of form which perfectly suited the material, but which continued to reflect Beaux-Arts traditions. This programme is pretty well self-contained, but you should look at Part Five before listening to it.

SET BOOKS

You will be asked to read several chapters from the following books: R. Banham, *Theory and Design in the First Machine Age*, Architectural Press (paperback), 1972; H.-R. Hitchcock, *Architecture: Nineteenth and Twentieth Centuries* (The Pelican History of Art), Penguin, 1971; N. Pevsner, *Pioneers of Modern Design*, Penguin, 1972. Many references are made to the A305 Course Anthology, *Form and Function*, ed. C. A. and T. J. Benton with D. Sharp, Crosby Lockwood Staples/The Open University Press, 1975, and to A305 D, *Documents*, ed. C. A. Benton, The Open University Press, 1975.

RECOMMENDED READING

The following books or articles provide background reading and should be fairly accessible:

Benevolo, L., *History of Modern Architecture*, Vols. I and II, Routledge and Kegan Paul, 1971.

Collins, G. R. and C. C., *Camillo Sitte and the Birth of Modern City Planning*, Phaidon, 1965.

Collins, P., *Concrete, The Vision of a New Architecture* (*A Study of Auguste Perret and his Precursors*), Faber and Faber, 1959.

Franciscono, M., *Walter Gropius and the Creation of the Bauhaus in Weimar*, University of Illinois Press, 1971.

Geretsegger, H. and Peintner, M., *Otto Wagner*, Pall Mall, 1971.

Giedion, S., *Space, Time and Architecture*, Harvard University Press and OUP (first published 1941 and frequently reprinted since).

Münz, L. and Künstler, G., *Adolf Loos*, Thames and Hudson, 1966.

Naylor, G., *The Arts and Crafts Movement*, Studio Vista, 1971.

Pevsner, N., *Academies of Art Past and Present*, Cambridge University Press, 1940.

Royal Academy of Arts, London, *Vienna Secession*, catalogue, 1971.

Sekler, E., 'The Stoclet House by Josef Hoffmann', *Essays in the History of Architecture presented to Rudolf Wittkower*, Phaidon, 1967.

Sekler, E., 'Mackintosh and Vienna', *Architectural Review*, Vol. CXLIV, 1968, pp. 455–6.

Sitte, C., *City Planning according to Artistic Principles*, Phaidon, 1965.

The Art Revival in Austria (*The Studio Yearbook of Decorative Art*, special issue), 1906.

The Studio, 1900–14, *passim*, has several articles on German and Austrian design (see particularly special issues).

Whittick, A., *European Architecture in the Twentieth Century*, Vol. I, 1950, Vol. II, 1953, Crosby Lockwood (both volumes reprinted with a third section, in one volume, Leonard Hill, Intertext, 1974).

Wiebenson, D., *Tony Garnier: The Cité Industrielle*, Studio Vista, 1969.

The following books and articles are of a more specialized nature. Many of them are worth tracking down for their illustrations alone.

Apollo, November 1971, special issue on Munich.

Bott, G., *Jugendstil* (catalogue of the Hessisches Landesmuseum, Darmstadt) Darmstadt, 1965, reprinted 1973.

Dekorative Kunst (especially for 1900–14, *passim*), Munich.

Deutscher Kunst und Dekoration (especially 1900–14), Darmstadt.

Deutscher Werkbund Jahrbuch (each annual volume is interesting, especially for 1912–15), Jena.

Gurlitt, C., *Zur Befreiung der Architektur im 19. Jahrhundert; Ziele und Taten deutscher Architekten im 19. Jahrhundert*, Bertelsmann, Gütersloh, 1969.

Hamann, R. and Hermand, J., *Stilkunst um 1900*, Akademie Verlag, Berlin, 1967.

Haus der Kunst, Munich, *Sezession Europäische Kunst um die Jahrhundertwerde*, catalogue, 1964.

Hoeber, F., *Peter Behrens*, Munich, 1913.

Hüter, K. H., *Van de Velde*, Akademie Verlag, Berlin, 1967.

Loos, A., *Sämtliche Schriften*, Vol. I, Herold Verlag, Vienna, 1962.

Mrazek, W., *Art Treasures in Austria—Art Nouveau*, Bad Voslau, 1968.

Muthesius, H., *Das englische Haus*, Vols. I–III, Wasmuth, Berlin, 1904–5.

Muthesius, H., *Cas englische Haus*, Vols. I–III, Wasmuth, Österreichisches Museum für Angewandte Kunst, Vienna, *Die Wiener Werkstätte*, catalogue, 1967.

Pevsner, N., 'Gropius and Van de Velde', *Architectural Review*, March 1963, pp. 165–8.

Posener, J., 'Hermann Muthesius', *Art Bulletin*, Vol. X, 1962, pp. 45–51.

Shand, P. M., 'Van de Velde to Wagner', *Architectural Review*, Vol. LXXVI, 1934, pp. 131–4.

Stephens, W. B., 'Victorian Art Schools and Technical Education', *Journal of Educational Administration*, December 1969, pp. 13–19.

Studio International, January 1971, special issue on the Vienna Secession.

Wagner, O., *Moderne Architektur*, Vienna, 1895.

Weber, H., *Walter Gropius und das Faguswerk*, Callwey, Munich, 1961.

Württembergisches Landesmuseum, Stuttgart, *Bernhard Pankok (1872–1943)*, catalogue, 1973.

As we made clear in the Introduction, this is a complex and extremely intricate period in many ways, with several apparently contradictory developments discernible. A measure of the problems facing us can be gathered from comparing the treatment of the period in the three set books for this pair of units, *Pevsner*, *Banham* and *Hitchcock*. Pevsner covers the period in one chapter (Chapter 7) and this is the climax of his book, binding together the separate strands laid out in his earlier chapters. For him, what happened in Germany up to the First World War in architecture and design represents the final triumph of reason and understanding which introduced the correct and universal architecture of the twentieth century. For Pevsner, this struggle was largely a question of abandoning the styles of the past, renouncing ornament and seeking to master and exploit the new materials dictated by industry. For him Gropius's Fagus factory is a completely modern building, not only because it retains nothing of the irrelevant styles of the past, but because it reveals a logical, structural use of materials, and, more than that, an imaginative use of these materials which aesthetically expresses the age. He counts among the steps towards this synthesis all the earlier work of architects who were either experimenting with new structural methods, or who were working towards a new, more abstract style. Thus we find, in Chapter 7, the French architects Perret and Garnier, the Americans Louis Sullivan and Frank Lloyd Wright, Viennese architects like Otto Wagner (and his pupils Olbrich and Hoffmann) and Adolf Loos, before Pevsner goes on to discuss the work of the Germans Behrens, Poelzig and Berg, with Gropius as the conclusion to the whole development. The suggestion in all this is that all these architects were instinctively working towards the same goal which, at its simplest, we can think of as expressed in Gropius's Fagus factory or his Model Factory at the Werkbund Exhibition of 1914 at Cologne.

It is hardly an exaggeration to say that one of the guiding principles of Banham's book was that this monolithic view should be eroded and replaced by a more complex assessment of the different factors and progressions of ideas. His main concern was to trace the sources for what he calls the 'Machine Age Aesthetic', while showing at the same time that the 'human chain of Pioneers of the Modern Movement that extends back from Gropius to William Morris' (*Banham*, p. 12 and the subject of Pevsner's book) belonged to an Arts and Crafts Movement which effectively terminated with the First World War. Where their approach can be most clearly contrasted is in their treatment of Futurism (*Pevsner*, pp. 210–11 and *Banham*, pp. 99–137). For Pevsner, Futurism lay on the fringes of the movement, like Expressionism, a tempting *cul de sac* from which the real pioneers like Gropius and Behrens steadfastly averted their eyes. Banham is also at pains to show the strong links with the past which marked the work

of Gropius, Behrens and the other architects before the war. He therefore groups in Section 1 (which is all about the academic heritage passed on to twentieth-century architects and designers—and not completely 'modern', therefore) all the architects discussed by Pevsner in his Chapter 7, with the exception of Frank Lloyd Wright and the Futurists. The suggestion here is that these architects were continuing nineteenth-century traditions rather than creating a totally new and completely successful twentieth-century architecture. But if you read *Banham* carefully, you will realize that his Section 1 does, in fact, make many concessions to the Pevsnerian thesis. He does not try to devalue the importance of the pre-war period. The main contrast is that he highlights different things and analyses the work of the main figures in quite different ways. The two books should really be read in parallel, in so far as that is possible, and considered as a dialogue. You should note that many of the same buildings and architects are discussed. These units will further modify the argument in certain directions, so it is important that you get the main ideas straight before you start.

Before you read the relevant passages from *Pevsner* and *Banham*, you should be aware of the way Hitchcock has handled the material, and of how you can make use of his treatment. Hitchcock decided to avoid some of the problems of organization created by isolating the 1900–14 period, by using a device which also tells us something about his views on the development of modern architecture. He isolates three 'generations' of architects, of which the first generation, born in the 1860s, were still active during our period. This enables him to follow through the work of these architects, many of whom lived to a ripe old age, into the twenties and thirties and beyond. Chapters 18–22 are therefore rather extended and break up the chronological sequence of events, since he has to keep coming back from the last works of one architect to the earlier works of another. The method does allow for clarification of some of the issues, however, and helps to make the book a very useful counterbalance to the others. In particular, Hitchcock helps us to keep the work of important architects like Frank Lloyd Wright and Perret, separate and distinct in our minds. You should read these chapters in your own time and at your own pace, familiarizing yourself with the material, so that you can consult Hitchcock quickly and effectively whenever you feel the need to 'check' or 'place' architects who are touched on in these units or in other set books.

Now, read *Pevsner*, Chapter 7 and *Banham*, pp. 9–97. Different people read at different rates, but you would probably have difficulty doing justice to this material in less than three hours. Some questions are listed below, to help you to sort the information out, and a commentary is added which notes particular things to look for. Do not allow yourself to get bogged down in this reading, but keep going fairly smoothly. You can, and should, refer back to difficult sections when you reach the appropriate points in the units.

While reading *Pevsner*, do not worry too much about the section on Frank Lloyd Wright and Sullivan; you will find that these architects will be dealt with very thoroughly in Units 7–8. When you read the passage on Endell, on page 194, you could stop and read the extract from the articles in *Form and Function* (no. 10). Please note, on page 203 of *Pevsner*, that the corners of the AEG Turbine Hall are not composed of 'heavy stone' as Pevsner suggests, as you will discover when you see the television programme, '*Industrial Architecture: AEG and Fagus.*' You will also see that the programme modifies Pevsner's view of the differences between Gropius and Behrens. On page 214, Pevsner wrongly refers to the supporting piers of the Fagus factory as 'narrow bands of steel'. The piers are of brick. You ought to think very hard, too, about the rest of his analysis of the coldness and austerity of Gropius's style and its relationship with machine production. On page 215, it looks likely, from recent research, that Hans Poelzig had been asked to design the machine hall in the first place and that Gropius and Meyer took over the commission at the last moment. How much of the design should be attributed to Poelzig is not yet clear, however. You will notice that Banham has a thing or two to say about this whole treatment of Gropius's work at the Werkbund Exhibition at Cologne (*Banham* pp. 85–7). Read this section in *Banham* when you reach this point in *Pevsner*, for contrast and comparison of the two different approaches.

Reading *Banham*, you must take account of the fact that he is trying to understand and explain what was well known at the time, but was in danger of being forgotten after the Second World War: that almost all the architects in this period were trained in some form of academic theory based, eventually, on nineteenth-century studies of the Classical and Gothic architecture of the past. There were many famous architects who had little formal training in architecture at all, like Van de Velde, Frank Lloyd Wright and Le Corbusier, but these men also picked up some of the axiomatic rules of planning and design which Banham talks about. So, although it might seem as though he is exaggerating the traditionalism of men like Behrens and Gropius, this must partly be seen as a corrective to the view which suggested that they broke almost completely with the past, and partly as an attack on the line of succession which Pevsner suggests through the Arts and Crafts movement and neo-Gothic architecture in England to Muthesius and the German Werkbund movement (which appears to be an anti-academic movement). Banham wants to suggest that the various theories of academic architecture provided the backbone for all the main developments, and that we have to understand how these worked if we are to understand the origins of the Modern Movement. You should read Chapters 1 and 2 carefully, to disentangle exactly which strands in the academic thought of the nineteenth century Banham considers important. Make sure you understand what he means by terms like 'elementarism' and 'rationalism', and how these relate to the writings of Guadet and Choisy. Notice how Choisy's views relate to those of Viollet-le-Duc and the other neo-Gothic champions, and how this helps to explain the ease with which the neo-Gothic architects like Labrouste and De Baudot accepted and exploited the new materials.

If Chapter 3 interests you particularly, you might like to start looking for the books listed as recommended reading under Perret and Garnier, to prepare for, or follow up, the radiovision programmes on the work of these two architects. In Chapter 4, Banham traces the conflict in England between the classical 'humanist' tradition revived by Geoffrey Scott, and the developed Arts and Crafts rationalism of Lethaby, which echoes Choisy's and Ruskin's writings. You should look at the extracts in *Form and Function* from Lethaby's writings. Chapter 5 is important not only for the treatment of the foundation of the *Deutscher Werkbund*, but also for Muthesius's theoretical standpoint, and in particular his 'keynote' speech of 1911, 'Where do we stand?' (*Form and Function*, no. 24). In Part Six we will discuss all this in greater detail, but you should read the extracts from Muthesius's speech, and some of the remarks made in the discussion of it. If you have time, read some of the other extracts from German writers in this period in *Form and Function*.[1] You will find that they will help establish the basic theoretical background. Many will be referred to specifically later in these units. Chapter 6 links in not only with Part Six in the section on industrial architecture, but also with the television programme on AEG and Fagus. Notice that Banham is suggesting on page 80 that Gropius lacked Muthesius's appreciation for transparency, lightness and mechanically adventurous forms, but that he was instead impressed by the strength and power of Behrens's factory buildings and chose the volumetric, solid and heavy forms of the Canadian grain silos as the best examples of industrial form. Indeed, Gropius chose the pen name 'Mass' for himself just after the war. But you could find examples of a greater awareness in Gropius's writings of the values of transparency and what he calls 'spirituality' of form, in these years. Notice, too, how Banham shows the connection between Muthesius's ideas and those of the Expressionists and even the Futurists who were influenced by the writings of Paul Scheerbart (pp. 81–3). This whole theme will recur in Units 9–10.

---

[1] See especially, nos. 17, 19, 20, 21 and 26.

Part 2 Arts and Crafts and the vernacular revival

1 Introduction

We have seen in Units 3–4 that in England, with some important exceptions, the Arts and Crafts Movement was intricately bound up with feelings of sentimental affection for the rural way of life, based on pre-industrial patterns of life and a pre-industrial use of hand labour and craftsmanship. In Germany, the Arts and Crafts Movement was sometimes referred to as *Dilettantismus*, which means more or less what it sounds like, amateurism linked to a strong moral feeling that the artist's and patron's duty was to revive the skills of craftsmanship even if it meant doing things with their own hands.

We shall look now at the vernacular end of the Arts and Crafts Movement, the wing which was most influenced by England and which expressed itself in the garden city movement. This body of opinion was vociferously represented all the way up to 1939 by the various preservation societies, which defended not only individual buildings of historical importance, but also the quality of the countryside and townscape. The national umbrella organization was the *Bund für Heimatschutz* (Society for the Preservation of the Homeland), but there were many specialist and regionalist organizations as well. We shall consider how broad the extent of this whole sphere of activity was, from large-scale town planning to the details of the reform of housing. Many people would say that much of the real work in the improvement of living conditions and the environment was carried out through these kinds of organizations, and we will probably find it increasingly difficult to make up our minds on this question as the course progresses. In the 1920s and 1930s, the *Heimatschutz* organizations bitterly attacked the Modern Movement, using arguments which, at times, stooped to depths of racialism only matched by the final glorification and inflation of this attitude under the Nazis. So we must try to sort out our ideas on the vernacular movement and see the virtue as well as the dangers inherent in the defence of the historic value of national and regional or local character. There was also the more tricky attempt to tidy up, rationalize and even standardize these same values to make reforms of quality and economy possible in twentieth-century social and economic conditions. What you must try and decide, as you read through this material, is how and why all these different elements were mixed in together and how, in each instance, we should try to distinguish (or indeed, if we should even try to distinguish) between, for instance, the search for the kind of simplicity characterized by the 'honest peasant's simple cottage', and the kind of simplicity resulting from scrupulous rationalization and stripping away of unnecessary detail. Both kinds of development are in full flood in this period, and both are extremely important for later developments.

2 Domestic architecture and town planning

As in England and America, architects, town planners and critics in Germany and Austria became increasingly interested in the problems of domestic architecture and housing during the nineteenth century. In fact the great majority of architectural discussions and publications were concerned with housing and town planning. There were two kinds of problems: comfort and hygiene, fresh air, greenery and moral and social problems on the one hand, and a home for the family, simplicity of life in countrified surroundings and changes in the symbolism of social class on the other.

There was a constant influx of English elements to Germany and Austria throughout the nineteenth century. The informality of the landscape garden had been imitated since the late eighteenth century. On the Continent, the name for this style of garden is, after all, *englischer Garten* or *jardin anglais*. In the 1820s, the importation of English cottage and villa designs began initially for summer chalets in princely gardens. But soon they were advocated by the middle classes, and by the middle of the century, the word 'cottage' was used to describe workers' model houses. At the same time, sociologists and politicians began to emphasize the political, religious and general moral importance of a stable family life, and the fact that every family should have its own house, or at least a self-contained flat. Again and again, attention was drawn to Britain: somehow the British had managed to keep this custom —often it was said because of the original Germanic ways of life which the Germans themselves had lost. Instead of houses in green suburbs, the Germans saw the growth of tenement blocks in all their cities. This was partly because many towns retained their old fortifications and boundaries throughout most of the nineteenth century, which forced architects to build concentrated, multi-storey blocks of flats, rather than expand laterally as had occurred in England. Most of the various attempts to create new kinds of suburbs on the lines of English villa estates in the 1860s and 1870s failed, mainly for financial reasons. Many of the new German cities maintained tenement blocks as the chief form for housing.

In the late 1880s, two new and radical developments set in. The first was concerned with the house and its interior, and more especially with the more complicated planning of middle-class villas. The influence came directly from England. The informality and the picturesque planning of Norman Shaw's houses were a revelation for German architects. From the interiors of the English Gothic Revival and Aesthetic Movement, the Germans took the lightness and practicality of the furniture. Thus in the early 1890s, a group of architects, mainly in Berlin, began to specialize in villas that strongly remind one of Norman Shaw's or Godwin's houses in the 1870s. If you compare Spalding and Grenander's Villa Maiano, Florence, of 1895, [**Fig. 1**], with Norman Shaw's Withyham, Sussex of 1866–7 (*Hitchcock*, Fig. 178), you will see how the influence was expressed. English firms began to sell furniture and fabrics in German department stores. It was unfortunate for the German designers, such as Ernst Eberhard Ihne (1848–1917) to be somewhat older than the pioneers of 1900, for their names are now almost forgotten. But the crusade for simplicity and the rejection of nineteenth-century ornament in German domestic design had its serious beginnings in the late 1880s and not around 1900, as it is often said.

The second development was the question of the finance and overall planning of housing for the lower classes. German town planners had learned a lot from Haussmann's Paris (cf. *Hitchcock*, pp. 195–203) since the structure of their towns was similar, with highly concentrated city centres. Baron Haussmann (1809–91) was the man mainly responsible under Napoleon III between 1853 and 1869 for the biggest effort of urban development in Europe. His basic aim, following the 1848 revolution and the rather insecure accession of Emperor Napoleon III, was to drive great radial boulevards and squares through the tangle of old and insalubrious working-class quarters in the centre of Paris,

to assure the public peace by the creation of large boulevards which will permit the circulation not only of air and light, but also of troops, [so that] the lot of the people will be improved, and they will be rendered less disposed to revolt.

(Haussmann, *Mémoires*, Vol. III, Paris 1890–3, p. 55)

Giedion devotes Part VII of his book, *Space, Time and Architecture* (recommended reading) to City Planning (pp. 641–79 on Paris and Haussmann's influence), if you would like to follow this up. Giedion also deals with the Garden City movement and looks at H. P. Berlage's plan for Amsterdam in Part VIII (pp. 682–707), for a rather different point of view to that expressed here.

In the last decades of the nineteenth century, German planners perfected the techniques of traffic planning, sewerage, bye-laws and so forth. In the late 1880s, they began to propose solving the housing problem by applying new bye-laws regarding density: if less density was allowed by reducing the height of tenement blocks for instance, people would live more comfortably and speculation and cost would be reduced. This was a new idea, since earlier attempts at a solution were chiefly concerned with health and financial matters only. In the 1890s, ideas of zoning were developed. The whole town was to be divided into various areas of different activities: factories, living quarters, parks and public buildings. The density of dwellings should decrease towards the outskirts of the town. But while some of the worst elements of the nineteenth-century town were removed by these measures, there was not enough finance from either private or public sources to

Figure 1   *Spalding and Grenander, Villa Maiano, Florence, 1895.*

really reform the system. Around 1900, several more radical remedies were proposed: public ownership of the land (influenced by the American reformer Henry George (1839–91) who based his egalitarian Single Tax and Land Nationalization schemes on the rapidly dwindling, wide open spaces of the American frontier) and migration from the towns to the country, where labour was supposedly needed. But, as in Britain, it was only after the First World War that massive public finance helped to create the vast garden suburbs.

In 1902, a tremendous enthusiasm arose for the English Garden City movement, after the publication of Ebenezer Howard's *Garden Cities of Tomorrow*[1]. German planners and architects flocked to Port Sunlight and later to Letchworth and Hampstead Garden Suburb. But the *Deutsche Gartenstadt Gesellschaft* (German Garden City Society), founded in the same year, took only the general idea, not the financial details, from Ebenezer Howard. In fact, while Howard's results were far from spectacular before World War I, the German movement was even less successful.

Large industrial combines, such as Friedrich Krupps's steelworks in the Ruhr, were influenced by garden suburb ideas in some of their housing estates, but most industrial housing was provided in the form of four- or five-storey tenement blocks. Krupps's Alfredshof (1894) and Dalhauser Heide (1907) were exceptions, but on too small a scale financially to be classed as genuine garden suburbs.

The only Garden City foundation of any consequence was Hellerau, near Dresden, largely Karl Schmidt's creation for his *Deutsche Werkstätten* (German workshops). If you look at the streets and houses of Hellerau [**Plate 1**] what strikes you first is the irregularity of the layout. The street line recedes and projects; few of the streets are straight. The houses, while simple in their lack of decoration, show a variety of gables and window sizes. The roofs are a markedly dominating element. The whole picture reminds you of an old village.

[1] This book was first published in 1898 under the title *Tomorrow: a Peaceful Path to Real Reform* and was slightly revised in its 1902 version.

We will come back to Hellerau in Part Four, in a different context, to show how some of Heinrich Tessenow's buildings go beyond this rustic simplicity to a more stark and geometric kind of order, based on a rationalized version of classicism. As pointed out earlier, the distinctions between the stylistic categories we are trying to establish are often extremely subtle. Garden suburb developments were planned occasionally throughout the whole period covered by this course. There were several between the wars, usually supported by the *Bund für Heimatschutz*, and the Nazis took up the idea, and some of the practice, in the 1930s. Staaken was a garden suburb development which was built during the First World War for workers at the Spandau armaments factory in Berlin [**Plates 2** and **3**]. Paul Schmitthenner was the architect and he combined some discreetly disguised tenement blocks with a picturesque town centre, cleverly designed to suggest an old village street composed of distinct, but joined, houses. The high gables and chunky, white painted windows in the street called 'Between the gables', as well as the use of vernacular materials such as brick and pantiles, echo the features of North German regional architecture. You will see some shots of this development in Television Programme 9, 'Berlin Siedlungen'.

3   The vernacular revival

It is quite clear that the development of the Garden City movement in Germany was intimately connected with a vernacular revival. Among all the new tendencies present around 1900, the vernacular revival was the one that went back furthest into the nineteenth century. Back in the eighteenth century, architects and patrons revived primitive peasant cottage styles for small houses in their gardens. In the middle of the nineteenth century, demands for rural simplicity were linked with the argument for simplicity and honesty of construction and we find a revival of brick and timber framing, shingling and other materials. Furthermore, the vernacular became a matter of stressing regional varieties in architecture, and an argument against the domination of some central school and a universal style. Regionalism had been strong in Northern Europe in many periods. Three main regional styles emerged through the second half of the nineteenth century: the Gothic type of construction of the Northern plains and the Baltic, the timber framing and mixed techniques of the mountainous and wooded parts of middle Germany, and rendered brickwork, which was the vernacular style of the South German plains, Swabia, Bavaria and parts of Austria. In each region, these developments gradually supplanted neo-Classical, Renaissance or other styles and continued well into the 1920s, and in many cases, through the Nazi period to the present day.

The most influential thinker in this context was Camillo Sitte, an Austrian architect and critic. In 1889 he published his book *Der Städtebau nach seinen künstlerischen Grundsätzen* (Town planning according to Artistic Principles). Sitte attacked the professional engineers and planners who had tended to control the planning offices in the nineteenth century. He disapproved of the creation of new town planning schemes by an over-rigid application of straight lines and patterns of streets marked in on a map, for reasons of traffic and hygiene only. He insisted that every planning project should show the elevations of the streets, and the perspective views at the major intersections. As Collins points out[1], this debate in a sense represents one of the recurring conflicts between the technically trained engineers and surveyors and the artistically based architects. Sitte was trying to revive town planning as an art, to recapture the sort of warmth, sense of scale and intimacy of the medieval and Renaissance towns and villages. For this reason, Sitte's book was also extremely influential for the preservationists and their associations. The *Bund für Heimatschutz* (Society for the Preservation of the Homeland) was founded in 1904, and from 1900 on, there was an increasing trickle of legislation, particularly by states such as Prussia and Hessen, designed to prohibit wanton destruction of old buildings and preserve the character of the countryside. In all this activity, attention was paid not only to outstanding works of historic architecture, but also to the humbler works of the vernacular. There were efforts to retain street frontages when new building was necessary, continuing the style and even the colour schemes of the original buildings. As with William Morris's 'anti-scrape' campaign in England, preservation led to a much more sensitive awareness of the value of simple houses, farmhouses and cottages, and this had an influence on the architecture of pre-war Germany, just as it had on the work of the English Arts and Crafts architects like Voysey and Baillie Scott. It is an interesting historical point, however, that in the 1920s and 1930s, the members of the *Heimatschutz* movement became the bitterest enemies of the Modern Movement, taking every possible opportunity to attack them in the press and in the planning departments. The members of the Deutscher Werkbund, which we will discuss in Part Six, were faced, after the war, with a deep-rooted split over the issues of whether to follow a reformist policy, based on the *Heimatschutz* principles (good, simple building in keeping with the surroundings using traditional materials and methods) or whether to allow the root and branch modernists to have their way. But that will be part of the story in Units 11–12.

In order to get the feel of the vernacular architecture of the central European countries, it would be a good idea to compare three houses all from the period 1900–7, to see what they have in common, if anything, and whether they are comparable to the Arts and Crafts houses in Britain which reveal some vernacular flavour. Hans Poelzig (1869–

[1] G. R. and C. C. Collins, *Camillo Sitte and the Birth of Modern Planning*, recommended reading.

1936) will be mentioned in these and later units on several occasions. The house he built for himself when he became the director of the Breslau Art School in 1903 is interesting, partly because of Poelzig's particularly confident handling of materials and forms, and partly because these forms do echo a certain amount of the vernacular style of that region [**Plates 4, 5** and **Fig. 2**]. Hermann Muthesius, whom we have encountered several times as the man who helped to put English Arts and Crafts architecture on the map, also built himself a house in Berlin between 1906 and 1907 [**Plate 6** and **Fig. 3**]. The last house we shall consider [**Plates 7** and **8**] was designed by Dusan Jurkovic-Sebrovic, around 1905, in Bohemia (now in Czechoslovakia). His house represents a more exotic form of vernacular architecture, closer to the forms you might expect to find in Russia than the western part of Austria–Hungary.

1 Is there anything in these houses which reminds you of the Arts and Crafts domestic architecture of Voysey, Baillie Scott or Mackintosh?

2 All these houses were among those selected by Hermann Muthesius in his book, *Landhaus und Garten* **of 1907[1]: what do you think he saw in them that might be relevant to the reforms he was seeking in domestic architecture?**

● 1 There are some forms in common with English Arts and Crafts architecture: the low-sweeping roofs and dormer windows, the lack of symmetry, the disposition of windows to suit the internal arrangements rather than the ordered rows, storey by storey; also, some of the features of the plans are similar. The Muthesius house is clearly larger and more formal than the Poelzig house, and the Jurkovic house is even more 'peasant-like' than anything we saw in Units 3–4, but, by and large, we can see some similarities with the more ornate houses of Baillie Scott and Voysey. In plan, there are also certain similarities. If you look at the Poelzig house plans [**Fig. 2**] you notice straight away that the main space is taken up by a staircase hall [illustrated in **Plate 5**], with a dining room opening off it in one direction and a seating niche in the other. Notice, incidentally, how clever Poelzig has been in running a little corridor between the window of this niche and the outside wall of the house, to allow servants to reach the front door out of sight of guests in the living rooms. This kind of central space, opening into subsidiary spaces for sitting or eating, was a feature we noticed particularly in the houses of Baillie Scott and was common in late nineteenth-century British architecture. In the interior of the Poelzig house [**Plate 5**] you can see an interesting mixture of very simplified forms, with a lot of white painted wood, but also crudely expressed structural details, like the screw-heads on the wood round the stairs. In the Muthesius plan, the arrangement of rooms is much more complicated, with the

[1] H. Muthesius, *Landhaus und Garten*, Munich, 1907.

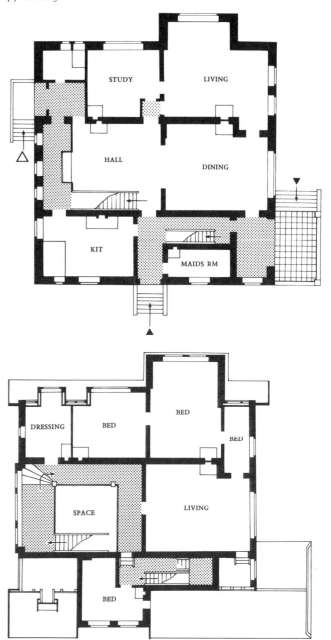

Figure 2 Hans Poelzig, own house in Breslau, 1904, plans.
(a) Ground floor

main living rooms spread over two storeys and two more storeys of bedrooms above them. There are one or two features taken directly from Mackintosh's houses: the staircase in a projecting, round-ended tower, with tall windows (like Hill House, Windyhill, or the 'House for an Art Lover'), or the rather splendid enclosed window seat on the first floor, next to the stairs, which is expressed on the exterior (as at Hill House) in a dormer window. Other features which we recognize from English Arts and Crafts houses are the little raised stage in the study on the first floor, and the use of a long service wing for the washing

Figure 3 Hermann Muthesius, own house, Nikolassee, Berlin, 1906, plans.

(a) *Ground floor*

(b) *First floor*

(c) *Second floor*

(d) *Third floor*

rooms and storage. Muthesius also used the upper floor of this service wing for his studio. The Jurkovic house is very different in most respects to the British tradition, relying mainly on wood for its construction and for its delightful decorative features. This kind of house has been built all over the eastern part of central Europe and Russia since the Middle Ages. The interior of the house centres on one big room with a ceramic stove, seating areas and a gallery all round leading to the bedrooms upstairs [**Plate 8**]. The informality of the living arrangements, based partly on the need to keep warm and lose as little heat as possible, is a little like some of the British cottage forms, but based on a completely different tradition. It is important to realize how different the vernacular forms of other countries are when one discusses the vernacular revival. Even the Muthesius and Poelzig houses could not possibly be mistaken for British houses, whatever similarities there might be in detail or general arrangement.

2   They are all houses which are decidedly not classical or close to any of the historic styles of the past and they are all designed for comfort rather than just for show. Muthesius was probably trying to bring together a group of houses (from all over Europe, incidentally, including several English houses from Bournville, Letchworth and Port Sunlight) which could be seen to be good, simple buildings, based on an understanding of the clients' needs and the appropriate methods of construction. He was not really after a revival of the vernacular (nor was Poelzig), but he did want to reform German housing and sought to do it by including examples, like the Jurkovic house, which were based on strong local traditions. His message is, we must learn to build as well as the country builder before we can try to undertake grander projects. •

The man who taught Hans Poelzig architecture at the Charlottenburg Technical University (the *Technische Hochschule*) was Karl Schäfer. Schäfer was particularly keen on medieval German architecture which he saw in constructional and rather mystical terms, and most of his better pupils went on to acquire a taste for expressionism in the 1920s. The other man who was recognized as one of the great architectural teachers of the turn of the century was Theodor Fischer (1862–1938), who taught at Munich (from 1908) and Stuttgart, before that. Eric Mendelsohn, Bruno Taut and Paul Bonatz were all pupils of Fischer and even the Dutch architect J. J. P. Oud worked in his office for a while. Fischer worked with the architects of the German Parliament building in the 1880s where he acquired a taste for massive but simple forms, and in the 1890s he spent some time in the office of the founder of the Bavarian vernacular revival, Gabriel von Seidl (1898–1913). If we look at his schools and churches of the late 1890s and early 1900s, e.g. his *Erlöserkirche* (Church of the Redeemer) in Munich of 1899 [**Plate 9**], we find an exceedingly picturesque composition. It is very asymmetrical and irregular by German standards of that time, especially for a church, but there is great simplicity in the treatment of the walls. All the openings are simply cut through the wall; there is no chamfering and little added ornamentation. The interior is equally plain, though its round arches are somewhat reminiscent of the Romanesque. As far as the identification with specific historical styles is concerned, the essential point of the vernacular revival is that it is seldom possible to spot elements of 'high' or 'textbook' styles; one has to look for the modest versions of the particular historic styles in remote parts of the country to find the sources. It is a conscious stepping down, a lowering of status, from the architecture of the 'architect' to the architecture of the builder and craftsman.

From this kind of attitude towards simplicity, a man like Fischer, with his mastery of constructional theory and his free-thinking approach to experimentation, could easily progress towards surprisingly inventive and daring undertakings. When we come to look at the work of Bruno Taut and Eric Mendelsohn, it will be worth remembering buildings like the Barracks church at Ulm, which Fischer built in 1912 with a reinforced concrete structure and a very powerful, if rather heavy style [**Plates 10 and 11**]. The exterior owes something to German Romanesque churches, which used to have a fortified tower block at the west end, and there are buttresses rather like a Gothic church, but the scale and brutality of the effect is notable. The interior is interesting for the way the reinforced concrete roof and balconies make the most of the constructional possibilities, achieving smooth and effortless sweeps. Clearly this kind of building can no longer be described as part of the vernacular revival, but it is clear that Fischer, like Poelzig and Muthesius and many of their contemporaries, was greatly influenced by the local building traditions and tried to live up to them, not by imitation, but by reinterpretation with modern means and with new ideas.

The vernacular revivals of the nineteenth century tended towards asymmetry, the picturesque, combating classical monotony and arguing the case for functional, individualistic variety in planning. As far as the overall form of small houses was concerned, the most important concept was that of simplicity. In the writings of the most important twentieth-century writers on the vernacular, Paul Schultze-Naumburg and Heinrich Tessenow, the concept of simplicity became so strong that variety was discarded altogether, and art and design were seen as concerns for a limited set of types. In this form, as in Tessenow's work at Hellerau, the vernacular was associated with a different set of ideas more closely connected with the revival of classicism. We will discuss this offshoot of the interest in vernacular simplicity in Part Four, but probably you can see from the examples illustrated that there was always a potential desire in the movement to aim at ever more austere simplicity, as opposed to the picturesque variety.

4   Neo-vernacular and National Romanticism

At this point, we shall briefly introduce the architecture of some of the smaller European countries, notably Scandinavia. To place this section in context, you should read *Hitchcock*, Chapter 24 (and in particular, pp. 531–40). Towards 1900, architecture became part of a wider cultural and political movement, the main purpose of which was to stress regional and national identity. As we have seen, it was fairly strong in countries which were already enjoying a high prestige, such as Germany and Britain, and in the case of a region, (remember Antonio Gaudí) Catalonia. But it grew all the more strongly in nations which were less happy and enjoyed a small degree of independence politically. Finland is the most striking example.

This country belonged politically to the Russian Empire until its independence in 1917 whereas culturally it depended to a large extent on Sweden. A strong movement stressing cultural independence in language, literature, history and art emerged in the later nineteenth century. It received more intense support when, in 1899, the Tsar withdrew many of the political freedoms Russia had granted Finland previously. The Finns themselves called their movement National Romanticism. In Denmark, the political reasons for turning towards cultural nationalism were less strong, but one must remember that Denmark had suffered badly in the wars with Prussia in the 1860s. The Danes also called their movement *Nationalromantik;* and the Swedes used the term *Nationalismen* for their own movements. 'Romanticism' is, of course, more difficult to explain. Here it means basically a stress on feeling as against nineteenth-century Rationalism, on primitive and symbolically powerful elements in folk art. Here the Scandinavians take part in the neo-Romantic and Symbolist movements spreading throughout Europe in these years. Thus, paradoxically, National Romanticism in Finland meant that the small and remote country for the first time really got in touch with the European, that is Parisian, Belgian and German *avant garde.* As far as architecture was concerned, there was the influence of the English Arts and Crafts, and more importantly, the influence of the American architect, H. H. Richardson and his simple, massive forms, and the American Shingle Style of simple, 'rural' domestic architecture (Hitchcock discusses Richardson and the Shingle Style in Chapter 15).

Denmark

Chronologically, we have to begin with Denmark, a country with a tradition of architectural experiment in the nineteenth century. One of the protagonists was Martin Nyrop (1849–1921) [**Plate 12**]. The main ingredients in his architecture were, the smooth brick surface of some of the medieval architecture of the Baltics, such as the Norwegian Stave churches, and a Richardsonian adherence to a tough and virile simplicity, using uninterrupted horizontals and massive masonry surfaces, while not giving up picturesque irregularity in planning. Copenhagen Town Hall, a project begun in 1888, is his major work. In his houses he sought to revive simple peasant types.

Sweden

In Sweden, Ferdinand Boberg must be seen as a close follower of Richardson (see *Hitchcock*, pp. 311–18), perhaps his closest in Europe. His fire station in Gävle [**Plates 13** and **14**] of 1890, contains many Richardsonian features including the low and massive rounded arches. Notice the Romanesque features (the round arches and columns in the windows, the massive towers and patterned brick) and the extreme richness of materials. In **Plate 14,** the use of rough

and smooth stone and light-coloured brick creates a very effective contrast of textures. Obviously, the picturesque qualities of medieval architecture have been considerably reinterpreted in this building. Ragnar Östberg's Stockholm City Hall, begun in 1905 [**Plates 15** and **16** and *Hitchcock*, Fig. 330], shows no direct borrowing from Richardson, but the brickwork appears smooth in surface and massive in outline and is effectively contrasted with sparse, but delicate decoration. There is a surprising austerity in the lack of mouldings where you would expect them, for instance round the big arches on the ground floor (*Hitchcock*, Fig. 330). The tower is treated in a very odd way, tapering towards the top. On the other hand, there is a lot of eclectic detail if you look for it, particularly in the interiors. It is important to realize what the emotional connotations of a building like this are and how it came to be considered among the most important buildings of its time. We always tend to restructure the history of the immediate past around our own tastes and preferences, under the guidance of the leaders of the Modern Movement. But the Stockholm City Hall seemed to many people convincing proof that the ability of architecture to create satisfying expressions of national character and focal points for city centres, was not yet dead. Arnold Whittick, writing in 1950, but calling on observations and recollections from the 1940s, devoted a whole section to this building and helps us to understand the way people could admire its eclecticism because of its emotional effect.

> . . . the most famous Swedish building of this period, the Stockholm City Hall, was an attempt at a full expression of a people, past and present, in architecture, sculpture and painting, suffused with all the romance that can be associated with national and local pride. If ever a building was a child of romance it is the Stockholm City Hall. . . . Many are the sources of the style of this City Hall. It is the result of a discriminating eclecticism combined with the creative genius of its architect. . . . Motifs taken from Greek, Roman, Byzantine, Romanesque, Gothic, Renaissance styles are all subjects of the architect and combined in the design.
>
> (Whittick, recommended reading, Vol. I, pp. 187–9)

The romantic quality of the building can be seen both in the exteriors, with a fantastic setting exploited to the full by a dramatic and heroic silhouette, and in the vast interior spaces, treated as a cleaned up, but still highly decorated version of Romanesque or Byzantine forms. If the treatment of surface is simple and even austere, the expressive language is humming with symbolism, designed to evoke Venice, Swedish castles and Byzantine or Romanesque churches and cloisters.

It was not only the countries which were going through the rigours of nationalist revival and self-identification, such as the Scandinavian group, which felt the need throughout the period (and to this day) of finding an architectural language which can express the direct and explicit symbolism of power and romanticism which this building conveys. One of the things we must watch out for in this course is not to underestimate the need for monumental architecture and to recognize the problems which later faced the Modern Movement, to meet the challenge of buildings like this in the field of major national monuments such as parliament or city buildings, museums or palaces of justice.

As far as domestic architecture was concerned, the Stockholm suburbs were closely modelled on English and American garden suburbs, and the houses show simple treatment with shingling. Again, if you look at Boberg's own house [**Plate 17**] in Stockholm, you can see how different the look of the Swedish vernacular is from British architecture. The way the roof tiles are brought right down to the top of the ground floor windows was based on the Swedish traditional use of shingles, rather as in American architecture. Much Swedish vernacular architecture was in wood. Do you remember Boberg's Swedish Pavilion at the 1900 Exhibition [**Plate 18**]? We noted there that wood allowed great formal freedom and these two buildings make an interesting comparison.

Finland

In Finland, two names must be mentioned. First Lars Sonck (1870–1950). His main work is the Cathedral of Tampere [**Plate 19**], designed during 1899–1901, with exceedingly massive, rough boulders facing many of the walls, a technique that evoked Richardson as well as the primitive medieval churches of Scandinavia. The crux of Richardson's influence is that his simplicity could be interpreted as primitivism. For comparisons, look at *Hitchcock*, pages 311–18 and Figs. 189–92. Better known was Eliel Saarinen (1873–1950), who later settled in America. In Finland, he mostly worked within the firm of Gesellius, Lindgren and Saarinen. Their first major work was the Finnish Pavilion at the Paris International Exhibition of 1900 [**Fig. 4**] which won them and Finland as a whole a great amount of recognition, in that it was both distinctive as a 'national' building as well as being in line with the 'Moderns' with its simple plan and large, dominating roof and Art Nouveau sweeping outlines. The firm then became chiefly known and publicized for their domestic work, which was highly original, leaning heavily on a local, rustic vernacular style [**Plates 20** and **21**]. Hvitträsk was an artists' colony for Saarinen and his friends in the countryside at Kirkonummi. The logs of wood used in their crudest structural form, that of the primitive log cabin, are formed into clean walls which somehow belie their rustic origins. The very simple horizontal windows, for instance, and the flat roof on the building in the centre, as well as the hollowed out spaces under the building on the right—all these things indicate that Saarinen and his colleagues were

taking a long, cool look at the structural possibilities of the material and coming up with a completely new treatment. The American Shingle Style had been producing similar results in the 1880s. As we have seen so often, the romantic attitude to the vernacular was often accompanied by experimentation into the basic principles of structure, simple and massive form and an original use of materials. The interior [**Plate 21**] shows this particularly, with a subtle mixture of the traditional virtues of the rustic Scandinavian vernacular, combined with bold formal expressiveness.

In 1904, Saarinen's firm took on and won the big competition for Helsinki central railway station, which Saarinen built between 1909 and 1914 [**Plate 22**]. Of all the large railway stations built during this period, this is one of the most sophisticated in its formal treatment. The basic logic of the treatment is classical, but instead of a specific historicist use of pilasters and entablatures, the surface is articulated in rebated strips, which seem to overlap and which are revealed at the corners. The treatment of the main arch is particularly good, using the size for dramatic effect, but not trying to create a classical formula for it. The main effect of the building is achieved by the finely detailed surfaces, the contrast between light granite below the darker stone which bands the roof of the transverse concourse building, and a very few pieces of carved decoration (notably the giant figures flanking the entrance and some tight patterned vertical mouldings set into the wall surfaces).

5 H. P. Berlage (1856–1934)

Some reservations must be made before we put Berlage in this context. He cannot be called a nationalist, nor did he explicitly support a particular vernacular style. Born in 1856, he was older than most of the 'pioneers' and he can be compared with Otto Wagner in Vienna (1841–1918), in that he had already established himself as an architect of nineteenth-century historicist styles. He drew mainly on the Renaissance, a source derived to some extent from his teacher, the renowned German architect, Gottfried Semper (1803–79), before he embarked on an innovatory course. Berlage thought and wrote a great deal about architecture in very general terms, continuing the theoretical tradition of Semper and Viollet-le-Duc. In conjunction with other architects and teachers in Amsterdam he evolved systems of proportioning, which seem to have had less effect on his own work than on that of others, especially that of the German architect Peter Behrens (1868–1940). Read *Banham*, pages. 139–47 and *Hitchcock*, pages 477–8 for rather different evaluations. The period of his activity that concerns us most here is from around 1895–1905. By the early 1890s Berlage had turned against classical architecture and the Renaissance and subscribed to Viollet-le-Duc's (and all the other Gothicists')view, that Gothic was the most appropriate model for a new style, since it was 'truthful construction'. What we have to strive for, he said, is 'honest construction in simplified form'. One of his first buildings in the new manner was the 'Nederlanden van 1845' in The Hague of 1895, an insurance office. The style of these buildings can be seen in the later Diamond Workers' Union Building (*Hitchcock*, Fig. 289). First of all he divests himself of classical regularity in most parts of the building by a varied composition, a lively outline, and a multitude of forms for the windows. The bare brick is dominant, and almost all the elements of ashlar decoration that remain, such as the corners of windows and the springing of the arches, are carefully contained within the brick surface; they neither project nor recede, but lie flush with the wall. What is thus emphasized is not so much the form or outline of these decorative elements, but the texture and colour contrasts between brick and stone.

The use of exposed brick had been revived since the middle of the nineteenth century with national and vernacular associations. But in most cases it had been subordinated to a basically classically derived framework of decoration, usually executed in a 'better' material: stone. But brick came to be seen more and more as containing positive aesthetic and symbolic elements, and in as far as Berlage encouraged this in Holland, he must be seen as an important contributor to the somewhat nationalistically-minded Dutch brick style of the twentieth century, most evident in the so-called Amsterdam School which we will look at later in the course. It must also be said here that these buildings are still Gothic in many ways, and that the Gothic elements have been taken from, among other sources, Viollet-le-Duc's illustrations of minor medieval domestic architecture.

Berlage's *magnum opus* is the Amsterdam Exchange, in construction from 1898 until 1908 [**Fig. 5**]. Red brick dominates the exterior and interior alike, but you can see from the detailed views how stone is used subtly for decorative effect. In the large interior halls [**Fig. 5a**], exposed iron trusses are used in a way more reminiscent of a railway station than a stock exchange building, although you should remember that there were many corn and coal exchanges in industrial Britain and Europe (Bunning's Coal Exchange, London, since demolished, is illustrated in *Hitchcock*, Fig. 111), which employed exposed cast- and wrought-iron structures internally. Viollet-le-Duc was again an important influence on the use of exposed iron in large public buildings. Looking at **Figures 5 a–b**:

1 **Which are the purely vernacular revival features of this building, particularly with respect to the use of materials?**

2 **Which features seem to you to go beyond the vernacular revival and appear to be of particular significance for later developments?**

Figure 4   Gesellius, Lindgren and Saarinen, Finnish Pavilion at the 1900 Exhibition in Paris.

Figure 5   Hendrik Petrus Berlage, Stock Exchange, Amsterdam, 1898–1908 (a) Main Hall (after 1909)

Figure 5   (b) Exterior

Figure 6   H. P. Berlage, house on the road to Scheveningen, The Hague, 1898, hall.

● 1   First of all, the insistence on brick as an indigenous Dutch material: brick was used extensively before the seventeenth century, whereas later, stone came to be used more and more up until the middle and end of the nineteenth century, to match the 'elevated' pretensions of classical architecture. Even in the nineteenth century, however, most minor buildings were built of brick, usually with plaster façades. Berlage's use of brick harked back to the seventeenth-century Dutch manner of building, the period of Dutch trading ascendency, but he made use of a great deal of stone for dressings which repays close inspection. The quality of the carving [**Fig. 5b**] is extremely original and not based on any specific prototypes. In general, apart from the use of materials, Berlage makes very few direct concessions to the styles of the past, using segmental arches for their structural convenience, in the internal arcades [**Fig. 5a**], but using a variety of different kinds of aperture on the exterior. Another element which is vernacular in a way, is the treatment of the windows to express interior spaces, however asymmetrical the effect on the exterior. In fact, this effect is controlled to a great extent, particularly on the main façade, but you can see in the windows of the flank of the building how Berlage allows the openings to come through where they are needed rather than lining up all the windows in regular rows.

2   The structural brutality of the interior, whatever the historical precedents, was to be of particular importance for the architects of the next generation. The large scale and impact of the whole building, not disguised by too much fussy detail, also provided a powerful challenge for later architects, rather like the Stockholm City Hall. Like that building, it had the kind of symbolic associations which the Modern Movement architects were often to be at pains to avoid, but the language of monumentality was of great importance for traditional architects in Holland and elsewhere. This building takes its place among the many

well known, powerful monuments to the new age of prosperity. To assess its modernity, you have to compare it to buildings like Horta's Maison du Peuple (Units 3–4, Plates 87 and 88), Mackintosh's Glasgow School of Art (Units 3–4, Plates 53–58 and 78–82) or Otto Wagner's Post Office Savings Bank in Vienna, which we will come to later in these units. ●

Let us look briefly at one more Berlage building, the hall of a house he built on the road to Scheveningen in 1898 [**Fig. 6** and *Pevsner*, Fig. 100] because it shows how the structural interest which Berlage picked up from his neo-Gothic masters was combined with a most adventurous technique. This little hall, with its complex arches and pendentives, reveals a fascination with brick structure and its many possibilities. The patterns formed by the different ways the bricks are laid, and the geometric compartmentation of space by the interlocking ribs, which create a 'hanging' oculus leading the eye upwards, reminds us rather of some of Gaudí's experiments with structural devices. In many ways it was buildings like this, developing further Viollet-le-Duc's curiosity about what could be achieved in structures, that foreign architects and Berlage's closest admirers at home learnt most from. We shall come across the offspring of this kind of scheme later in these units and in the course.

Part 3   Jugendstil, Sezessionstil and the Viennese contribution

1 Introduction

So far we have been looking at developments in Europe which correspond more to the Arts and Crafts Movement in Britain than to the development of the Art Nouveau in France and Belgium. But there was an Art Nouveau style which flourished in Germany which was referred to as *Jugendstil*, after the periodical *Die Jugend*, which was founded in 1896 (see film strip frames 1 and 2). You have come across references to this wing of the Art Nouveau style in *Pevsner* and in the radiovision programme, 'The Magazines of Decorative Art', which illustrated a poem by Victor Hardung with a page layout designed by Bruno Paul (Radiovision booklet, Programme 2, Fig. 11). Also illustrated is an Otto Eckmann page from *Pan* from 1895–6 (Radiovision booklet, Programme 2, Fig. 12). Both designers were members of the so-called Munich group, which also contained Behrens, Endell, Riemerschmid, Obrist, and Pankok. We will come across most of these artists later in these units as designers, but the important thing to recognize straight away is that they mostly conformed to the British, Belgian and French model by beginning as painters or graphic artists (Obrist, like Dresser and Gallé had studied botany) and turned to design and architecture under the influence of Ruskin and Morris and the Arts and Crafts Movement in England. The links with Belgium and France (Meier-Graefe founded *Pan* in Germany but visited Van de Velde in Uccle as well as having his shop in Paris) were important because the Art Nouveau phenomenon only really manifested itself in design in Germany after 1897 and was heavily influenced by France, Belgium and Britain. Van de Velde moved to Germany in 1899 and was an important influence when he exhibited in Dresden in 1897, alongside other designers from Bing's Salon de l'Art Nouveau group.

From the beginning, the *Jugendstil* movement showed a split between the highly ornate and curvilinear forms derived from nature (Eckmann, Obrist and Endell are the most obvious examples), and a harder, tougher decorative vocabulary which is more abstract and closer to Van de Velde's forms by this stage. For Endell, in fact, there was a curious ambiguity, as Pevsner points out (Set book, p. 194) because as well as designing the most exuberant of all decorative schemes, his Studio Elvira (*Pevsner*, Fig. 122) he was also working on a theory of abstract proportion based on supposed laws of perception rather similar in origin to Van de Velde's own (cf. *Form and Function*, no. 10). This is important because almost all the *Jugendstil* designers quickly worked their way through the Art Nouveau phase to become the leaders of the rational design movement in Germany headed by the Werkbund, which will be the subject of Part Six in these units. Almost without exception, they were advocates from the start of a restrained vernacular style in architecture, similar to that of Poelzig and Muthesius [cf. **Plates 4–6**] or Van de Velde (Units 3–4, Plates 89–92 and 104–5). There were few architectural examples to match the work of Guimard or Horta.

To see the kind of range typical of most of the *Jugendstil* architects, we could take the example of Bernhard Pankok (1872–1943). He studied sculpture and painting in Dusseldorf, Berlin and Munich and was one of the young artists working on *Pan* and *Die Jugend* from their foundation. During 1896–7 he turned to applied art, designing furniture with powerful, chunky forms and a certain amount of vegetable form in the ornament. He met and formed a working partnership with Bruno Paul and exhibited a room with him at the 1900 Exhibition in Paris (also the 1902 Exhibition in Turin), which you saw in the television programme on the 1900 Exhibition. From 1902 he lived and worked in the art school in Stuttgart. He was one of the founder members of the Deutscher Werkbund and although he was always more involved with painting, the graphic arts and hand-made furniture, he did play his part in the attempts to design for mass production, producing several interiors for Count Zeppelin's fleet of airships after 1911. He even made several designs for aluminium tube chairs for these airships, which were unfortunately carried out in wood.

Pankok's Art Nouveau phase was most clearly expressed in his graphic design and furniture, but a house he built for the art historian Dr Konrad Lange in Tübingen [**Fig. 7**], shows the use of Art Nouveau ironwork and a graceful and simple version of the kind of picturesque forms Guimard used in his houses in France (Radiovision booklet, Programme 4). Clearly, though, there is nothing reminiscent of Art Nouveau in the overall form of the house and you would have to look at the details of the carving on the upstairs balcony or on the stone piers to find any real Art Nouveau flavour. Inside [**Fig. 7b**], the treatment is austere and crisp, with slight inflexions in the forms of the chairs and table, and an Art Nouveau frieze along the wall, but little more than that in the way of Art Nouveau detail.

Figure 7   Bernhard Pankok, Lange house, Tubingen, 1901.
(a) Exterior

Figure 7 (b) Interior

During 1905–6, Pankok designed a building to house eight studios for the Stuttgart *Verein Württemburgischen Kunstfreunde* (Württemburg Society of Art Lovers), of which Pankok was a member [**Fig. 8**]. The surprising starkness and simplicity of the exterior, with its huge window walls which project above the roof line in greenhouse-like dormers, shows how rational and precise he could be when faced with a functional and necessarily cheap commission. This studio building should take its place among a group of art school buildings all over Europe, from Glasgow to Weimar, which show a desire to experiment with tough forms and a clean use of surface and glazing. Works like this were more important for later developments than the many delightful Art Nouveau graphic designs and pieces of carved furniture which Pankok and his generation produced between 1897–1902.

Figure 8 Bernhard Pankok, studio building for Verein Württemburgischen Kunstfreunde, Stuttgart, 1905–6, street elevation.

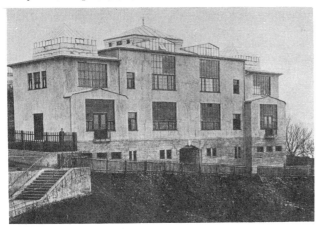

The same phenomenon can be seen in the Viennese version of the Art Nouveau epidemic, the Secession style. Here there was even less out-and-out voluptuousness of the French or Belgian kind, and a style of clear, graphic decorative forms, based far more on the square and the circle, was developed which can quickly be seen as a reaction to Art Nouveau, as much as a part of it. Again, you have seen examples of the early phase of the Secession style in the radiovision programme, the pages designed by Olbrich and Hoffmann (Radiovision booklet, Programme 2, Figs. 14–17) for *Ver Sacrum*.

We have left out a detailed examination of the flowering of *Jugendstil* in Germany and the early phase of the Secession style in Austria, because it is important to concentrate on the main developments of the pre-war period and because you already have a good idea of what Art Nouveau forms look like, from Units 3–4. If you would like to refresh your memory of Pevsner's treatment of the Secession style and *Jugendstil*, look up pages 105–6 and 193–202 in your set book. If you want to follow this up with some further reading, *Sources of Art Nouveau* by S. T. Madsen has a useful summary and a good bibliography.[1]

The main aim of this part of the units is to see how German and Austrian architects and designers developed from their Art Nouveau phase, and to see how important other influences were. We will come across elements of Art Nouveau decoration in many of the works illustrated, but the main issues turn on more complex questions than whether or not these things are Art Nouveau. One of the main reasons for this is that the grip of classicism, in various forms, and the vernacular revival was very strong. For this reason we are beginning with Vienna, and the work of Otto Wagner, who managed to make many startling innovations while remaining firmly within the main canon of classical and academic architecture.

2 Vienna: background to the 1890s

It is important to realize the background to the Viennese developments at the end of the nineteenth century. Austria's cultural relationship with Germany had been ambiguous from the time of its separation from Germany and even more so from the period of complete independence following the foundation of the Second German Empire in 1871. There were still many ties with Germany, but on the other hand, Vienna was the centre of a large empire itself. Its importance was greater than that of any of the German centres, including Berlin, which only in the later nineteenth century began to exceed Vienna in size. Like Germany, Austria, or at least Vienna, enjoyed a rapid economic development. This was accompanied by a feeling for cultural advance as far as the visual arts and architecture and design were concerned, especially since it was felt that little development had been shown in Austria during the first half of the century.

[1] S. T. Madsen, *Sources of Art Nouveau*, George Wittenborn, New York 1956.

In 1857 the Emperor, Franz Joseph II, decreed that the old fortifications, which surrounded the old city and proved a barrier between it and the new parts, should be razed and replaced by the *Ringstrasse*. This ring-road is a grand boulevard lined by the houses of the nobility and grand bourgeoisie and by many splendid public buildings culminating in the museums and the Imperial Palace. Whereas the façades of the palaces and the rich apartment blocks are decorated with the nobler versions of Neo-classicism and the neo-Renaissance, the style of the public buildings varies: a Gothic town hall, Gothic churches, a Graeco-Roman Parliament, neo-Baroque theatre and so forth. On the whole the *Ringstrasse* is one of the most interesting ensembles of later nineteenth-century architecture. In *Hitchcock*, on pages 212–17, there is an account of this development which you should consult now. Until the end of the century the decorations grew more exuberant and only after the mid 1890s, under the guidance of Otto Wagner and his pupils, did a new movement emerge. As far as the applied arts were concerned, Austria was the first country on the Continent to officially 'reform' its arts and crafts (in the 1860s), by systematizing the way they were taught and by showing carefully selected historical examples in a museum for applied arts. But Austria was also one of the last major countries to show the influence of the new movements in the 1890s. Two events were instrumental in changing the outlook among Austrian designers: the foundation of the Secession and the change of directorship in the Museum of Applied Arts (then the *Österreichisches Museum für Kunst und Industrie*). The *Vereinigung Bildender Künstler Österreichs* (Austrian Fine Arts Association) of 1897 was a breakaway group of young artists who adopted the term 'Sezession' from earlier groups of this kind in Germany. The motto of the Secession was: 'Der Zeit ihre Kunst—der Kunst ihre Freiheit' which means something like: 'each period ought to have its own art—freedom for the arts'. It is the same concept that we will find in Otto Wagner's book, *Moderne Architektur*, (recommended reading), the compulsion of the *Zeitgeist*. From the start, the Secession included a number of architects and designers, some of them still working under Wagner, who was a kind of father figure to the Secession. The second event, the appointment of A. von Scala as director of the museum, meant a complete change of outlook for the most important institution of Austrian applied arts. Von Scala had previously been Director of the Oriental Museum where he had developed a keen interest in Japanese art. He began his activity with the Christmas exhibition of 1897, where he showed English furniture; not many recent examples, but rather the simpler furniture of the eighteenth century. Vienna came under the grip of English fashion. 'Everything smart the Viennese are now calling English', wrote Adolf Loos in 1898. It was in that year, with the first exhibition of the Secession and the first Viennese Art Nouveau

designs in the *Österreichisches Museum*, that the new movement really began in Austria. The enthusiasms of this young group were encouraged by Baron Felician Myrbach. He was appointed director of the *Kunstgewerbeschule* (School of Applied Arts) in 1899 and one of his first jobs was to appoint Koloman Moser (1868–1918) and Joseph Hoffmann (1870–1956, a pupil of Wagner) to the teaching staff. Both these designers were conscious of the clarity of English design and the wide field of applied art that English artists and designers were involved in. Already in 1897, Hoffmann had said

it is to be hoped that soon the time may come for us too, when we will be able to buy wallpaper and ceiling paintings, not to mention furniture and household articles, from the artist, not the dealer—England is far in advance of us here.

And the time did come, with the establishment of the *Wiener Werkstätte* (Vienna Workshop) in 1903. Before looking at some of this design work we shall consider the architecture of Wagner, Olbrich and Hoffmann in Vienna, for many of the new ideas were first realized in the buildings and only later in design.

3   Otto Wagner (1841–1918)

During the first fifteen years of his career Otto Wagner was one of the many successful designers of flats and offices in the Vienna *Ringstrasse*. Wagner was born in 1841 and after studying at the Vienna Polytechnic he went to the Berlin *Bauakademie* (Academy of Building), in the early 1860s, which was still a stronghold of classicism and eclecticism derived from its most famous teacher, the Prussian Neo-classical architect K. F. Schinkel. When Wagner began to design in Vienna, his leanings were much more strictly classical than those of most of his German contemporaries. He certainly stood under the spell of Gottfried Semper, the most eminent German interpreter of classical and Renaissance architecture in those decades, who crowned his career with numerous grand public buildings in Vienna in the 1870s (*Hitchcock*, Fig. 133). Wagner must also have been looking to France with its deep-rooted classical tradition and the more rational academic interpretation of architecture which was later embodied in Guadet's great treatise (*Banham*, Chapter 1). Apart from his private commissions, Wagner took part in many competitions for major public buildings throughout Europe, where he enjoyed pulling out all the stops of grand classical decoration. In a similar vein he designed stage-set decorations for numerous festivities, such as the marriage of the Crown Prince.

Wagner moved to the top of the architectural profession in Vienna by becoming Professor of Architecture at the Academy of Fine Arts. But for him this was not a position for advocating the continuation of classical traditions, but a platform to propagate something that seemed radically new. In 1895, he published his opening speech in a little book entitled *Moderne Architektur*. Its most important message is that architecture should orientate itself to 'modern life'. The nineteenth-century practice of imitating the styles of the past is totally inadequate. He draws an analogy between architecture and men's fashions; the latter are already expressions of modern life, in their simplicity and in their unity, and it would be inconceivable to walk around the streets in the costume of Louis XIV. In the late nineteenth-century, modern forms in architecture should be simple, of 'almost military' uniformity. Another word for modern life is 'realism'—for him 'modern' painting is realistic painting (as against the predominance of the historical and mythological subjects of the earlier nineteenth century), and he cites English domestic architecture and the Paris exhibition buildings of 1889 as examples in architecture. Form follows construction, he maintains. Using new materials should lead to a new style more or less automatically. Wagner's book is generally hailed as the beginning of modern architecture, at least in Austria, but its main element seems to be precisely its rhetoric, its confidence and its radical language. In its arrangement and in its contents it is quite a traditional book. The three Vitruvian elements of solidity, commodity and beauty are there. The question of an appropriate style for the nineteenth century had been asked for many decades, and the issue of deriving new forms from new materials had been aired for a long time. Little is said about what the new forms should actually look like, and Wagner admits that the few hints he gives are derived from the classical tradition: symmetry, the emphasis on the horizontal line, the flatness of the wall, the use of flat, slab-like cornices.

Architects of the nineteenth century and the Modern Movement have been accused of being 'advanced' in their thinking and writing, but lagging behind when it comes to putting their ideas into brick and mortar. Wagner's buildings of those years and the following decade, however, appear as a clarification of his ideas in *Moderne Architektur*. His output grew rapidly, partly because a great deal of designing was done by his pupils. His most important commission involved supervising the construction of the track and stations of the *Stadtbahn*, the urban transport in Vienna. Begun in 1893 and carried on until around 1904, there are few precedents for such an utilitarian job being undertaken by such a respected member of the profession. Wagner must have considered it an important job himself since he included some illustrations of it in the second edition of his book [**Fig. 9**].

The Unter-Döbling station is a typical example of Wagner's mixture of classicism and technical brutalism. The sides of the little station are executed in classically detailed stone, while the central canopy and the internal

Figure 9   Otto Wagner, Stadtbahn station, Unter-Döbling, Vienna, 1895–6.

areas reveal the supporting iron trusses quite naturally, using decorative forms worked into the structure itself. The most significant elements, with hindsight, are the iron parts. The fact that iron is used for this type of building is not new, of course, but the way it is used is. On the whole, the iron parts of the bridges and other structural parts are more exposed and they seem bulkier and visually more satisfactory and chunky than other nineteenth-century structures. The fact that iron construction looked too thin and spindly had been an aesthetic reproach since the middle of the nineteenth century. On the other hand, where iron is used more decoratively in Wagner's stations, especially on the series of small stations, it is treated like the stone and plasterwork, with the same strict linear patterns and Neoclassical ornaments. It seems that the linear qualities of the material are emphasized, and it might not be too far-fetched to see this as a parallel to Horta's ironwork of the same period.

A building which shows Wagner as directly susceptible to the new decorative influences coming from the rest of Europe is the so-called Majolika Haus, one of a pair of blocks of flats with shops below, in a suburb developed just outside the *Ringstrasse* in Vienna [**Plates 23, 24** and film strip frame 3]. The overall form of this building, constructed in 1898, is similar to hundreds of basically classical blocks in Vienna, but Wagner devised a surface treatment of coloured majolica tiles, echoed by the sunflower motif on the balconies, to decorate the wall surfaces, instead of the usual applied classical detail. The weaving, spreading floral motifs justify us in bringing Art Nouveau into the discussion, but there is little here to compare with mature Art Nouveau architecture like that of Horta or Guimard. It looks as if Wagner took the opportunity of the new decorative ideas arising from the Secession to do away with the main classical repertory of forms, finding a much cleaner, more stripped way to handle the window openings, the balcony supports and so forth. The real value of this building is that it probably helped Wagner to see how to make a new start and rid himself of the baggage of ornament carried by all the buildings since the redevelopment of the *Ringstrasse* in Vienna. It is debatable whether Wagner was further prompted in this direction by the most brilliant of his pupils such as Olbrich and Hoffmann, whom we will be looking at shortly.

There were other examples in Vienna at this period which showed a comparable or greater abstraction of form, which seems to have emerged from a general feeling that the excesses of the *Ringstrasse* architecture should be counteracted. Max Fabiani, for instance, built commercial premises for Portois and Fix in one of the suburbs outside the old fortifications of the city which are as stripped and austere in their treatment as anything Wagner was to achieve [**Plate 25**]. The lower two storeys belonged to the shop, with its workrooms and storerooms, while the upper floors were rented out as apartments. Like Wagner's Majolika Haus, the walls were surfaced with tiles, but treated in a simple geometric patterning which incorporated the intitials of the firm at the top left hand corner, but were otherwise devoid of display or ornament. Only the cornice was decorated with a rippling moulding which we will find again in some of Hoffmann's buildings. This was Fabiani's first building and his later works tended to be more complex in articulation, although equally sparse in ornamentation. Despite the impact of Secession decoration and the continuing influence of various forms of classical decoration, there was a steady trickle of buildings of this kind by architects in Wagner's circle, many of whom were indeed his pupils. But for the sake of clarity, we will look now at some of Wagner's later buildings before returning to the work of his pupils.

Wagner's most famous building and one of those which crop up in most discussions about key early modern buildings, is his Post Office Savings Bank, 1904–6 [**Plate 26** and **Fig. 10**]. A large and imposing building which takes up the whole of a block (the second half of it was only completed in 1912, in basically the same style), the exterior [**Plate 26** and **Fig. 10**] is startling both from a distance and close to. Although there are several classical elements in the composition, and some rather pompous statuary at roof level, the treatment of the façade is very original, with no overtly classical detail and a decorative treatment which relies on thin sheets of stone fixed on with large exposed aluminium bolts. The statues at roof level [**Fig. 10**] were also cast in aluminium. The canopy of the main doorway is supported by thin cast aluminium posts and cantilevered brackets and looks completely fresh and original even today. But it is the interior which is usually illustrated [**Plates 27–30**]. The main hall is the central space in the court around which the building is deployed. The curved glazed ceiling is supported by a framework of ties which hang from a second, glazed pitched roof above. The vertical stanchions, which help to support this structure, pierce the lower glass ceiling and support the main horizontal girder to which the aisle roofs abut. The effect is of an amazingly clear and

Figure 10   Otto Wagner, Post Office Savings Bank, 1904, cut away elevation.

luminous simplicity, as if the skin of glass were held up by magic. The flattened curve of the ceiling is particularly important in creating this effect because it seems so different from our idea of what a self-supporting roof should look like. **Can you see evidence [in Plates 27–30] that Wagner was deliberately exploiting the aesthetic mood he had achieved with his structure, in the decorative treatment of the hall?**

● The very light tone of the wall surfaces, which are faced with marble and white opal glass up to a height of about eight feet or so [cf. **Plate 28**], echoes and increases the impression of brilliant luminosity. Also, the aluminium sheathing of the stanchions and the extraordinary decorative heating shafts [**Plates 29** and **30**], add to the exotic whiteness of the imagery. The very precision with which the glass is framed, with crisp glazing bars, is matched by the extreme simplicity of the wall treatment. Decoration is limited to the use of an extremely discreet chequer border around most of the wall openings, taking the place of any mouldings, and an equally sparse delineation on the floor. The double lines in the glazing bars of the ceiling, which correspond to where the stanchions pierce the skin of glass, are met by brackets supporting the girder along the outer walls [**Plate 27**], echoed by the heating shafts, and picked up by a grid of lines on the floor [**Plate 28**] which mark out all the divisions of the space in a most clear and positive way. ●

Every detail of this building is worth studying as a sign of how architects in the future were going to try to replace the need for employing mouldings and complicated detailing everywhere, to articulate surfaces and spaces, by using the simplest and most subtle means. Wagner used slick, lustrous surfaces of plaster, marble and glass, and he exposed the bolts attaching these to the fabric. The glazing bars and the mechanical accessories like heating shafts and lights are emphasized. German architects, and Walter Gropius in particular, must have studied this building closely, and borrowed ideas from it in the handling of surface materials and detailing.

Another work which shows Wagner's masterly handling of surface was the pair of apartment blocks at the corner of Döblergasse and Neustiftgasse, 1910–12 [**Plates 31** and **32**]. In the doorway of No. 4 Döblergasse, we can not only see again his use of aluminium facings for decorative effect (on the door), but the way he echoed this with the glazing bars of the staircase window and the horizontal ribbing, in stucco, of part of the façade. By this stage, Wagner was developing quite personal and independent ways of decorating and dividing up his wall surfaces. In **Plate 32**, you can see that, despite the basically classical treatment of the cornice, the wall surface is marked out with thin lines scored in the stucco, as if the wall was faced with plates of

marble, while the decorative borders are carried out in black glass dashes and dots. The horizontal strips below are also made up of inset black glass as a version of the stucco ribbing we saw in **Plate 31.** An important element in the Viennese contribution to modern architecture was in this kind of confident abstract decorative treatment, very slick, sophisticated and a little precious. We will find reminiscences of this kind of elegant simplicity in much German architecture in the years which followed. Wagner was particularly influential because his architecture rested on a solid basis of logical and restrained classicism. In the second villa he built for himself, designed in 1905 and built during 1911–12 [**Plate 33**], we can see this strange Viennese mixture of the classical form, complete with a coffered cornice and a classically ordered arrangement of windows, stripped of the normal classical detailing, but furnished instead with a sumptuous detailing of an abstract kind. The surface of the wall is stuccoed and inset with shiny coloured terracotta tiles to form borders and rhythmic arrangements. This villa, like the Majolika Haus and aspects of the Post Office Savings Bank, raises the question of Wagner's indebtedness to his pupils and the Secession style, so we must go back to 1897 and the founding of the Secession to look at their work.

4   J. M. Olbrich in Vienna

To see what the possible influence of Olbrich on Wagner was, we should start by comparing the *Stadtbahn* station by Wagner at Unter-Döbling [**Fig. 9**], with one of the stations where Olbrich almost certainly did the designing in Wagner's office, the Karlsplatz station, 1898–9 [**Plate 34**]. We can note the cheerful sunflower motif and the decorative treatment of the metalwork in the latter. The whole little pavilion is framed in iron and faced almost entirely in sheet iron, which itself makes a considerable contrast with the Unter-Döbling station. But in general, the decorative forms of this little station (there are two pavilions like this, one on either side of the road) remind one most of the Majolika Haus flats by Wagner of the same period. To see Olbrich's style more clearly, we should look at the Secession building, 1897–8 [**Plate 35**], which Olbrich designed while still working in Wagner's office. It is worth reminding yourself of Olbrich's graphic style in his *Ver Sacrum* illustrations (Radiovision booklet, Programme 2, Figs. 14, 15 and 17). An example of his interior decoration designs which are very closely based on the *Ver Sacrum* designs, can be seen in film strip frame 4.

Immediately after its foundation the Secession began to plan its own exhibition building. In its plan and general arrangement, the Secession building did not differ much from the customary buildings of this type, a somewhat shed-like agglomeration of spacious halls, with an entrance façade crowned by a dome squeezed between four supports

[**Plate 35**]. But the formal treatment of the main façade shows a strong influence of Wagner's concept of flat wall surfaces and sharply projecting cornices. Olbrich, in fact, develops a more three-dimensional, volumetric treatment, compared to Wagner. Olbrich then goes further than Wagner at this date in abandoning almost all the conventional classical decoration, be it Neoclassical or neo-Baroque which the early designs for the Secession building still show. He replaces them with plant forms, more precisely trees, moulded into the stucco facing of the building at the corners. Unlike the Majolika Haus, these trees do not grow freely up the façade, but are squeezed into more or less straight outlines which are in turn conditioned by the arrangement of the architectural forms. The open-work, gilded metal dome creates the most unexpected effect and the general massing is very good. In the following years the influence of the overall curved forms of international Art Nouveau became stronger. In his villa of 1899 for the art critic Hermann Bahr, near Vienna, Olbrich attaches some three dimensional floral ornaments to the corners of the eaves, which created rather strange curves in conjunction with the high pitched roof, and the rather 'cosy' contours of the house. In 1889, Olbrich was called to Darmstadt to be the chief architect in the *Künstler Kolonie* (Artists' Colony) and we will come back to him later.

5   Josef Hoffmann (1870–1956)

Josef Hoffmann and Olbrich were the best known designers to come out of the Viennese Secession. Slightly younger than Olbrich, Hoffmann had a rather slower start to his career. Like Olbrich he also worked in Wagner's office and when Olbrich left Vienna in 1899, Hoffmann stayed to become professor at the School of Applied Art from where he exerted a strong influence on design in the whole country. His graphic style emphasized bold, decorative forms, clearly differentiated from each other (Radiovision booklet, Programme 2, Fig. 16). The Viennese Secession magazine, *Ver Sacrum*, contained many illustrations of this kind by Hoffmann, Olbrich and others. His first designs of any note were some of the interior fittings and pieces of furniture in the Secession building in 1898, very simple carpenter-like pieces with lattice-like decorations. As in Olbrich's case, the influence of international Art Nouveau grew stronger in the following year, but already in some of his designs for the Austrian exhibits at the Paris International Exhibition of 1900, he abandoned all curves in favour of completely square outlines, with no emphasis on the cornice and smooth surfaces, relying on the careful treatment and polish of the surfaces and the contrast of materials such as metal and glass.

Here we have in fact already the main components of the mature Secession style in furniture. Its origin must be traced

to a combination of many sources: Wagner's simplified classical style, his insistence on clear horizontal and vertical lines, the furniture of the Empire period (or as its vulgarized version is called in the German speaking countries, *Biedermeier*), which was very much in fashion in these years and which Wagner and Loos and many others professed to like. It is also likely that Hoffmann came under the influence of Loos, who produced some designs of this kind slightly earlier. There was also Baillie Scott's simpler furniture. From 1900 onwards, Hoffmann and Mackintosh exchanged their views about furniture, which had become quite similar. Mackintosh was celebrated as a hero when he came to Vienna, and Hoffmann also visited Mackintosh in Scotland.

Hoffmann's first building of any size was the Villa Henneberg outside Vienna [**Fig. 11**] begun in 1900. It is on the one hand a curious compromise between whimsical

Figure 11   Josef Hoffmann, Villa Henneberg, near Vienna, 1900. Plans and elevations.

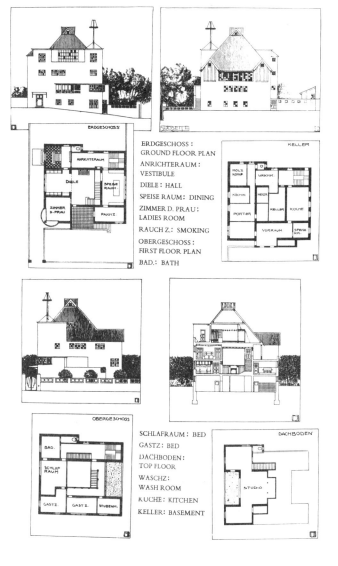

ERDGESCHOSS :
GROUND FLOOR PLAN
ANRICHTERAUM :
VESTIBULE
DIELE : HALL
SPEISE RAUM : DINING
ZIMMER D. PRAU :
LADIES ROOM
RAUCH Z.: SMOKING
OBERGESCHOSS :
FIRST FLOOR PLAN
BAD.: BATH

SCHLAFRAUM : BED
GASTZ : BED
DACHBODEN :
TOP FLOOR
WASCHZ :
WASH ROOM
KUCHE : KITCHEN
KELLER : BASEMENT

7 J. M. Olbrich at Darmstadt

The repertoire of the Darmstadt style can be assimilated from Olbrich's poster for the 1901 Exhibition [**Fig. 13**]. The Viennese chequerboard is there, and the same geometrical abstraction of natural forms which we saw in the Secession building. If you look at two of Olbrich's pieces of silverware designed specially for the exhibition [**Plates 39 and 40**], you can see how these correspond to the forms in the applied art designs. Both the candlesticks and the tea caddy employ amethysts as decorative motifs and there is something here of the techniques of Mackintosh or Ashbee, who loved to set off points of translucent colour against smooth polished surfaces. The candlesticks have a definitely anthropomorphic element, like stylized figures holding up the candle-holders with outstretched arms. The forms in both pieces are closer to the Art Nouveau than most of the work of Olbrich and his colleagues at Darmstadt, but we can see another example of restrained Art Nouveau curves if we look at a chair by Patriz Huber (1878–1902), designed for the Glückert house in the Darmstadt colony and made by Glückert's furniture workshop [**Plate 41**]. **In what ways are the three objects [Plates 39–41] closer to Art Nouveau than the forms in the poster [Fig. 13]?**

● The chair has the kind of organic structural form which we saw in Art Nouveau furniture, with a rib connecting the front legs to the back in a smooth transition. The chair looks like a cool and restrained version of a Van de Velde chair. The two Olbrich designs use curving decorative forms and there is a sort of living organic softness to the surfaces, compared to the hard abstraction of the poster. Olbrich moved away from this kind of Art Nouveau as time went on. ●

Olbrich laid out the whole Matildenhöhe site with great care, and almost all the buildings were designed by him. The most important one was the workshop and exhibition building, called the Ernst Ludwig Haus [**Fig. 14, Plate 42** and film strip frame 5]. Like the Secession building it is a rather shed-like structure, only more so, since it has really only one façade. Although long and low in its general arrangement, it shows a more vernacular treatment of its parts, with long unbroken walls with undisturbed horizontals and a sharply projecting roof, reminding one of Austrian alpine buildings. Most of the ornament is concentrated round the central doorway [**Plate 42**] behind a great semi-circular arch which reminds us of Hoffmann's drawings in *Ver Sacrum* (Radiovision booklet, Programme 2, Fig. 16). The painted and gilded stucco decoration in the arch too (film strip frame 5), comes straight out of the forms developed in *Ver Sacrum* (Radiovision booklet, Programme 2, Fig 14). The main part of the exhibition was, however, a street lined with villas, mostly the family houses of the artists' colony. They adhere to two basic types: the narrow type with large pitched roofs, irregularly placed windows with small panes, mostly derived from the English Domestic Revival [**Fig. 15**], and a type developed by Wagner and Hoffmann and having a touch of the simple Italian rural house. The Villa Habich is a bit like Hoffmann's Henneberg house [**Fig. 11**] with its emphasis on the square block of the house with

Figure 14   (b) *Plan of Matildenhöhe site, Darmstadt, 1900.*

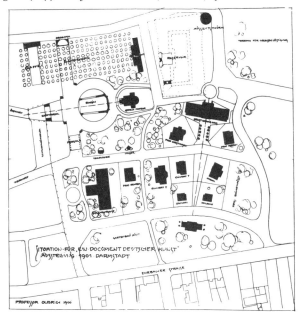

Figure 14   (a) *J. M. Olbrich, Ernst Ludwig Haus, Darmstadt, 1901.*

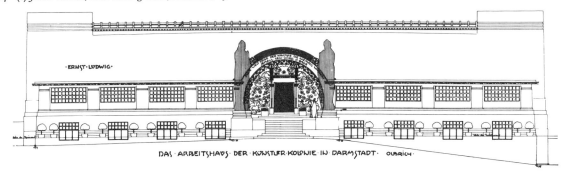

Figure 15   J. M. Olbrich, Villa Deiters, Darmstadt, 1901.

Figure 17 J. M. Olbrich, ingle-nook in his own house, Darmstadt, 1901.

Figure 16   J. M. Olbrich, L. Habich house, Darmstadt, 1901.

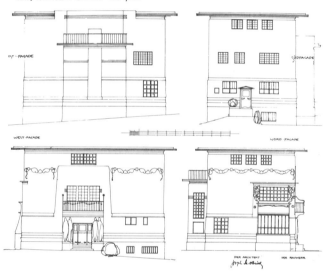

hall has a bold and rather brash painted decoration. Notice the peacocks' tails on either side of the fireplace, lined with electric light bulbs. The familiar Viennese chequer motif seems almost out of place here. A similar quirkiness can be found in the strangely adapted inglenook in his own house [**Fig. 17**]. Mackintosh's influence is quite clear here, in the white lacquered wood and thin, nervous proportions.

Olbrich's work in the following years until his early death in 1908, though growing in volume, is less significant in this context. The most outstanding achievements of the Darmstadt colony were, as indeed in the Secession as a whole, the simplification of the forms used in design, tending towards geometrical shapes, and in the revival of interest in craftsmanship and the nature of materials. As we have seen, there was also great freedom of expression. The pavement [**Fig. 18**] that runs between the artists' houses at Darmstadt, made out of small flat cobbles, forming a black and white linear geometric design, sums up this attitude; it also provides a unity and conformity to the total artistic environment.

In 1907, Olbrich designed the Hochzeitsturm (Wedding Tower) as a crown to the Mathildenhöhe site [**Plate 46**]. There is a whole range of projects for this design, but the final version, with the motif of a five-fingered hand raised in benediction at the top, and the use of bands of windows asymmetrically placed so that they run round the corners, was to be most influential later on in the most unlikely quarters. Gropius probably had this in mind when he designed his Chicago Tribune Tower competition entry in 1922 (*Banham*, Fig. 107).

8   Peter Behrens at Darmstadt

Peter Behrens (1868–1940) was the other major designer at Darmstadt and his work in these years should be briefly introduced here. Born in Hamburg in 1868, son of a

larger windows, sudden projection and a flat roof extending far out over the walls [**Fig. 16**]. The Glückert II house is a compromise between the two [**Plates 43–45**]. If you look carefully at **Plates 43–45,** you will see the diversity and richness of Olbrich's decorative technique. The roof, window and door shapes are subtly related to modulations and patterning of the stuccoed wall surfaces [**Plate 43**]. Notice the tree designs moulded onto the stucco, and the row of flower-like (or bubble-like) forms cut into the plaster above the horizontal socle. In **Plate 44,** you can see these forms treated rather as in *Ver Sacrum*, as repeated patterns stamped out, as it were, like a printed or stamped border on textiles or wallpaper. The three-quarter circle entrance arch and door seem more oriental than Art Nouveau. In the interior, which has been completely restored after Olbrich's original drawings [**Plate 45**], the central staircase

Figure 18   J. M. Olbrich, pavement in the artist's colony, Darmstadt, 1901.

Figure 19   Peter Behrens, The Kiss, 1897.

Figure 20 Peter Behrens, own house, Darmstadt, 1900–1.

(a) Ground floor plan

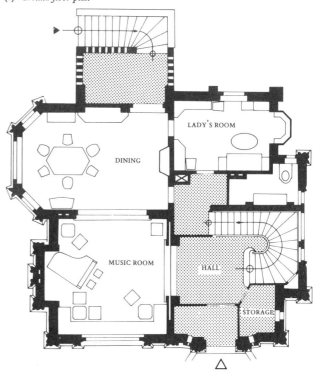

landowner, he studied painting in Düsseldorf and then settled in Munich. He was one of the founder members, as an artist and illustrator, of the Munich Secession in 1893, the first of the German breakaway groups of young artists. Around 1897, he rapidly moved away from painting towards Arts and Crafts production: graphics, and flat pattern designs such as *The Kiss* [**Fig. 19**]. In 1899 he was called to Darmstadt to be a member of the Artists' Colony.

His contribution to the 1901 exhibition was his own house. Although a smallish villa on a compact plan [**Figs. 20–24** and **Plate 47**], it tries, in complete contrast to Olbrich's picturesqueness, to be as ordered and rigid as possible. But there is a curious imbalance in the exterior, between a free interpretation of vernacular forms and a sort of illogical structural rationalism. Brick and green terracotta mouldings are used to create the semblance of logical form in emulation of the vernacular forms found in the Baltics, which Behrens admired. But he worked them out in a purely decorative way. The bands of green terra-cotta tiles create a strange rippling effect, almost like the stem of a rose against the rectilinear brick. Behrens carefully studied the fall of light to create these effects and they

Figure 20 (b) First floor plan

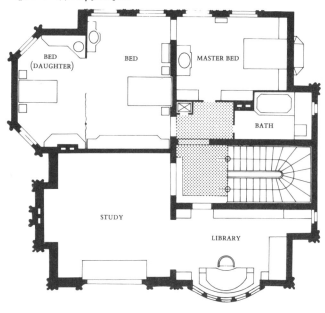

Figure 21 Peter Behrens, own house, Darmstadt, 1901, music room.

Figure 22 Peter Behrens, own house, Darmstadt, 1901, dining room.

repay close observation. There were many examples of this kind of wavy moulding in Vienna [cf. **Plate 25**] and Behrens may have seen it there. Inside, the music room [**Fig. 21**] is the centre of the house; it ends in an apse with an allegorical painting and a grand piano. The walls are covered with blue glazed mirrors and the ceiling is gilded. You will notice that although there are still some curvilinear elements of Art Nouveau present in the dining room [**Fig. 22**], the forms used are, on the whole, much more simple and more in keeping with the sort of work being produced in Vienna. The chairs are like Van de Velde's Bloemenwerf chairs of 1895 (see Units 3–4). Their form is clean and simple, with clear sweeping lines. The whole room, with the repeated Sheraton oval motif (English

eighteenth-century furniture had been admired for its clarity and quality and exhibited by the Viennese from 1897 onwards), has a unity about it that is reflected in the crockery [**Plate 48**] where the angular plan of the articles is offset by repeating the curving linear motif in the decoration. These, along with other crockery produced by Behrens at Darmstadt, are printed in pure primary colours on white. Not only are the pure colours far removed from the 'lingerie subtlety' of many Art Nouveau ceramics, but the actual forms are harder and more geometric than most Art Nouveau designs. Van de Velde at times ventured into this sort of pattern, partly under the influence of the German designers.

If you now look at the lady's room in the same house [**Fig. 23**] many more rectilinear forms are being used: the table has an angular aggressiveness about it that might tempt you to say that it had been shaped by a machine rather than by hand; the settle fits neatly and geometrically into the corner. The carpet is almost Cubist in its geometric abstraction.

This same geometric element, which is to be found in Mackintosh's later work, can be seen in the illustration of Behrens's design for his own house (film strip frame 6). The letters at the bottom are set within rigid rectangles that take the letter forms away from the undulations of Art Nouveau, even though the readability of the letters is hardly increased by the defining lines. Despite the laurel leaf border to the poster (cribbed from Olbrich and Vienna) there is a rigidity in the placing of the building on the page. The white areas are allowed to come through as a positive part of the design. The front door of Behrens's house, and the cover for Nietzsche's *Thus Spake Zarathustra* [**Figs. 24** and **25**], show how Behrens linked the curvilinear and the geometrical together. The overall form is laid out in the most rigid way, but a slight softening of contour is allowed, which gives it great rhythm and life. Behrens did

Figure 23   Peter Behrens, own house in Darmstadt, 1901, lady's room.

Figure 25   Peter Behrens, cover for Nietzsche's Thus Spake Zarathustra, 1902.

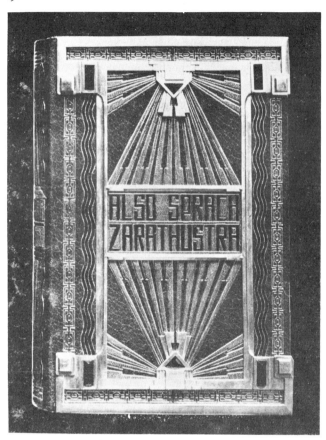

Figure 24   Peter Behrens, own house, Darmstadt, 1901, front door.

Figure 26   Peter Behrens, Typeface for Alexander Koch's publishing firm, 1902.

ℬ𝔦𝔢 Zukunft unſerer Induſtrie wird mit davon abhängen, ob wir entſchloſſen und im Stande ſind, der nächſten Generation eine ſorgfältige künſtleriſche Erziehung des Auges und der Empfindung angedeihen zu laſſen. Bisher haben wir nur für die Ausbildung von Künſtlern geſorgt.   Alfred Lichtwark.

also design a type face [**Fig. 26**] for Koch's publishing firm, and this too has a right-angled order about it. Nevertheless, this was in part due to the punch cutters, which perhaps helped to reinforce the idea that geometric forms go hand in hand with machine production. **As well as the strong influence of the Viennese designers in the use of geometric forms and pure colours, what other elements do you notice in Behrens's designs?**

● We have already noted a strong English influence on the Viennese artists, and this element is still evident at Darmstadt where it was transmitted not just via Vienna but via periodicals and the close association of Koch with England. Arts and Crafts elements are especially noticeable in the beams and the emphasis on quality and unity. There is, however, an extremely exotic quality to Behrens's interiors. For him, the house is not just a place for family accommodation, but a kind of sanctuary where art and life are combined and integrated. His decorative schemes may seem very strange to us, but he drew on many vernacular forms which were more familiar to his contemporaries. This can be seen in the slightly medieval impression which the house (and typeface) make, which was soon to be replaced by a more classical quality. ●

9   The Wiener Werkstätte

In 1901, Hoffmann and Koloman Moser organized an exhibition in Vienna which consisted of a series of furnished rooms, some designed by themselves, others by Ashbee and Mackintosh. Unlike the English public, the Viennese thoroughly approved of the furniture they saw, and much of it was sold. Partly as a result of the success of this exhibition, Hoffmann and Moser decided to go to England to study the methods of the English designers, and the way they organized their workshops. While in England they were especially impressed by Ashbee's Guild of Handicraft workshop at Essex House, where he had managed to produce good, simple designs, relatively cheaply, by bypassing the middle man. Hoffmann also met Mackintosh in Glasgow. On their return to Vienna, Hoffmann and Moser decided to try and develop a similar workshop in Vienna, where they could attempt to bridge the gap between artist and craftsman in their desire for unified simple designs. Ruskin and Morris were their spiritual guides. This idea was realized in 1903 when the Wiener Werkstätte was founded. Like the Darmstadt Artists' Colony, it was partly due to the encouragement, as well as the financial backing, of a Viennese businessman, Fritz Wärndorfer (who had also patronized Mackintosh), that the whole project got off the ground.

At first Hoffmann and Moser found a small workshop and employed three workmen, but they soon found it necessary to move into larger premises. Hoffmann and Moser did all the designing, which included bookbinding, leatherwork, gold and silver work, lacquer work and cabinet making, not to mention the complete design of buildings.

What were the main criteria involved in the designing they were doing? Much can be gained from looking at the work programme they published in 1905 (cf. *Form and Function*, no. 18). In this programme, their main criteria were usability and truth to materials; for example, they wanted to make use of the wood grain in furniture and show it off as wood, indulging in the beauty of the texture. They had no desire to produce cheap work, for they felt (judging by the cheap articles then available) that it was produced at the expense of the worker. They had a rather condescending attitude towards machinery.

We should also like to draw attention to the fact that we too are aware that, under certain circumstances, an acceptable article can be made by mechanical means, provided that it bears the stamp of manufacture, but it is not our purpose to pursue that aspect yet. We want to do what the Japanese have always done and no one could imagine machine made Arts and Crafts in Japan.
(J. Hoffmann and K. Moser, First catalogue of the Wiener Werkstätte, Vienna 1905)

There had been a few attempts in Austria, by artist-designers to work with industrial manufacturers, but these had been fraught with difficulties. These difficulties were especially apparent in silverwork, where the manufacturers had firstly been used to getting designs for nothing (by members of the firm, who had no specific design training), and secondly, were used to selling the articles for the price of the weight of the silver, regardless of the design. Why should they change their methods? Their only gain would be more administrative work and higher costs for the public.

Look at some of the objects produced by Hoffmann. The office desk and chair of 1905 [**Plate 49**] is made of stained and polished black oak, with a white colouring to bring out the grain of the wood. The forms are geometric and skids have been added to the lower part of the legs to emphasize the regularity of the form. **Compare this desk and chair with Mackintosh's furniture illustrated in Units 3–4, Plates 48–52. What are the similarities and differences?**

● In both designers' work the quality of workmanship and the clarity of form are important, but Hoffmann emphasizes and simplifies the geometric aspects much more than Mackintosh. Mackintosh uses plain black or white and right-angled forms in some pieces, but he usually includes a floral motif or introduces curves somewhere. Hoffmann adapted many of Mackintosh's ideas to the more sophisticated Viennese idiom of absolutely minimal form. The comparison highlights the individualism of Mackintosh and the more developed, abstract taste of Hoffmann, which was at least in part due to the more advanced public understanding in Vienna. ●

The clock by Kolo Moser [**Fig. 27**] made of ebony and beaten silver with ivory hands, is similar in basic form to a classical temple and the actual face of the clock is a perfect square. The materials used are of a slightly precious nature. The importance of materials for Hoffmann is shown very clearly in the cigar box [**Fig. 28**], with its vine scrolls and large stones (which resemble techniques used by the Viennese painter, Gustav Klimt). Moser likewise emphasizes the same elements in his work; you only have to look at the vase and sugar basin [**Plate 50**] designed by him in 1905, to see the similarity in approach. Like Olbrich, Moser sets semi-precious stones off against smooth surfaces, but here the forms also are pure. Incidentally, it is worth comparing the bowl with Christopher Dresser's metalwork designs (Units 3–4, Plates 19–21). There does seem to be a slightly different approach, however, in Moser's designs

Figure 27   Kolo Moser, clock in ebony and beaten silver (Wiener Werkstätte), 1906.

Figure 29   Kolo Moser, glassware executed by Baka Lowits and Sons, Vienna.

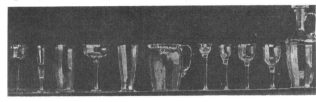

Figure 30   Josef Hoffmann cutlery, silver and steel, (Wiener Werkstätte), 1905.

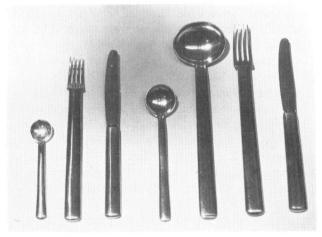

Figure 28   Josef Hoffmann, cigar box in silver set with semi-precious stones (Wiener Werkstätte)

in glass [Fig. 29]. He had spent six months in a glassworks before the Wiener Werkstätte had been founded, and therefore did have some experience of machine production. This experience is reflected in his own designs for glass; he evolved a system of making the glass in one piece, rather than in three separate pieces, as was the usual practice, and of making wine glasses and tumblers the same size. This is probably one of the first examples of a designer in Austria intelligently approaching a design problem in a functional way, for the uniformity of size would aid packaging and transportation of the glasses, and making them in one piece would reduce the number of processes involved in manufacture, and thus probably the cost of the article. Hoffmann's cutlery designs [Fig. 30] seem much more precious by comparison, and closer to Mackintosh's. Formalism seems more important than practical utility. By 1906, the Wiener Werkstätte had become so large and successful that it became necessary to farm out some of the work to other workshops. They had succeeded in their aims of reviving craftsmanship and quality in designed objects (elements which were part of the Arts and Crafts tradition), and also in popularizing this concept among the fashionable people in Vienna. They had also established the vogue for clean, pure forms that can be equated with the classic simplicity of an expensive object. Except for a few isolated cases, like Moser's glasses, and some bentwood furniture, redesigned by one of Hoffmann's pupils and made by Thonet (who had been making mass-produced bentwood chairs since the middle of the nineteenth century) there had been no attempts to come to grips with the machine, nor was there any desire to. Like the other Arts and Crafts manifestations, the main emphasis was on the problems of the artist or a designer, rather than looking to the designer in industry.

In order for there to be a total change in style and quality of design, it was not sufficient just to train artists and art teachers, which is what applied arts schools were doing. The trade schools and manufacturers had to be made more aware of art, since it was against the machine-made objects copied from historical styles that Morris and likewise the Wiener Werkstätte were reacting. Technical schools for training workmen had been in existence in Austria since the mid-nineteenth century. They were originally founded by the Ministry of Commerce and Trade, but had been taken over by the Department of Education in the 1880s and then thoroughly reorganized and made more art-orientated at the turn of the century. Different schools specialized in different subjects, from cabinet making and locksmithing, to weaving and jewellery, depending on the speciality of the area. The students were between twelve and sixteen years old, but classes for older manufacturers took place on Sundays and in the evenings. The main purpose of the schools was to train workmen both in the technical and commercial aspects of their trade and in the application of art to manufactured objects. Although, following the English tradition, the source of much of the decorative design was nature (miniature zoos existed in some schools), the Vienna museum provided books and patterns which could be adapted and copied to make the designs more simple and up to date. Most of the teachers in these schools had been trained in the School of Applied Arts and, as in the Birmingham school, it was mostly a matter of teaching the pupils neoclassical forms. Many of the students came from remote villages where there was a strong tradition of peasant art, and some of this was reflected in the work as well.

10   The Palais Stoclet and Hoffmann's later houses

Hoffmann's *magnum opus* is the Palais Stoclet [**Plates 51–55** and **Fig. 31**], a very large villa in the outskirts of Brussels, begun in 1905. It was built for a Belgian financier, who had lived in Vienna at the time of the foundation of the Wiener Werkstätte. If you look at the plan [**Fig. 31**], you will see how close this is to Mackintosh's 'House for an Art Lover' design of 1901–2 (Units 3–4, Fig. 40). It departs to a large extent from the influence of the British Domestic Revival in its decorative treatment, in its relatively symmetrical arrangement and in the fact that the roof is given much less prominence. But in its arrangement, with its repetitive series of small windows, with the lack of emphasis on the cornice or roof line, it does not remind

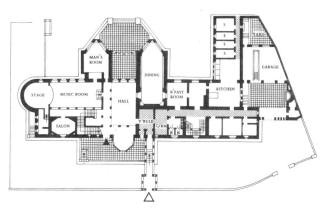

Figure 31   Josef Hoffmann, Palais Stoclet, Brussels, ground plan.

one much of the classical Viennese villa type either. The main decorative feature on the outside is the metal moulding, a kind of cyma, which runs round all the window frames and lines the edges of the wall surfaces including the roof line [**Plate 51**]. Each compartment of the wall appears thus as an isolated unit. The walls themselves are covered with carefully cut slabs of thin Norwegian marble. It is the brilliant whiteness of the exterior, accentuated by the rippling metal mouldings and block-like massing, which marks the exterior out. The building culminates in a tower terminating in a group of gilded sculptures. This adds to the character of pretentious preciousness that is conveyed by the whole of the exterior treatment, and which, of course, is the main element in the interior [**Plates 52–55**]. The Palais Stoclet was designed to show off and enhance without distraction the many works of art that Adolphe and Suzanne Stoclet collected and treasured. It was also designed to entertain, among others, the artistic and intellectual élite of Europe, both casually and more formally, with performances in the theatre-cum-concert room.

The Stoclets had admired Hoffmann's work in Vienna, and having just inherited a large sum of money, they decided that he was the man to design them a palace which would have the quality, the atmosphere and the expensive elegant simplicity necessary for the comfortable contemplation of the arts. All the furnishings were hand-made by the Wiener Werkstätte and Stoclet refused to disclose the cost. Look carefully at the plan of the Palais Stoclet [**Fig. 31**], and the interiors [**Plates 52–55**].

1   How is the Palais Stoclet laid out and what sort of quality does it have?

2   How far does it follow the ideas developed by the Wiener Werkstätte?

● 1   You enter the house by a covered passageway placed centrally on the façade. This leads you both physically and psychologically from the main boulevard to the front door. Inside the front door is a small entrance room, completely white: a moment of meditation before entering the vestibule [**Plate 52**]. Here the walls are *verde antico* marble with square white niches in which are gilt vases, carefully silhouetted by top lighting. The axis of the shallow-arched barrel vault with its black-edged squares is mirrored in the black marble line in the floor. The glass doors to the right lead to the service rooms, kitchen, cloakroom, etc., also all in white. The glass doors to the left lead into the great hall, and thence to the other reception rooms, the music room, dining room, men's room, salon and terrace. The great hall [**Plate 53**] is two storeys high, with a gallery that seems to float around two sides of it. Slim square-section marble piers extend from floor to ceiling, and the white panels of the gallery (with no visible means of support) emphasize the geometric play of horizontal against vertical. The hall is the heart of the building: it pulsates with reflective surfaces of polished wood, glass and marble, light and airy in the daytime, glowing by artificial light at night. The rest of the rooms are darker. The dining room [**Plate 54**], probably darkest of all, has the glowing Klimt mosaics *Expectation* and *Fulfilment* running along either side of the long walls, which are covered in a honey-coloured marble veneer. The lower third of this wall has a unit of dark *Portovenere* marble shelves alternating with highly polished wood doors. In this room the precise attention to detail and quality of workmanship is especially evident. Look at the way the Klimt frieze fits exactly into the wall, slightly raised from the marble at the bottom and neatly trimmed by a band at the ceiling line. Nothing has been left to chance, from the placing of each unit within the room to the awareness of the impact of one material on another. Each room at this end of the house is furnished and decorated deceptively simply, but retains a sumptuous quality and preciousness in the use of highly reflective materials. The same elements may be seen in the rooms at the other end [**Plate 55**], cloakrooms, children's rooms, etc., but on the whole, more white is used here, both in the furniture and on the walls. However, this white never appears either bland or stark: it suggests a highly styled clean and precise dignity.

2 In a way, the building sums up the approaches and attitudes of the Wiener Werkstätte. In everything there is a self-conscious emphasis on simple geometric forms, from the designing of some of the furniture to the basic inter-locking of the shapes of the rooms. For example, the planning of the first and second floors is based on a twelve foot square. There is a totality and unity about the relation-ship of the rooms to each other, yet each has its indivi-duality. The quality of the different reflective materials is emphasized by their simple forms and the fact that they have a unique and precious quality. •

The following points sum up the house's importance:

1 the use of simple geometric forms in a stylized manner

to enhance the nature of the sumptuous materials;

2 the emphasis on the quality of workmanship, combined with restraint in ornament;

3 the creation of atmosphere and mood;

4 the successful combination of geometric simplicity with individuality.

After the Palais Stoclet, Hoffmann moved more and more towards the kind of highly cultivated and mannered classicism which came to distinguish much Viennese design until the war and beyond. This foreshadows the material we will cover in Part Four, but it is interesting to see how smoothly Hoffmann made the transition to avowed classicism and how much of his abstract formalism and decorative mastery remained. The Primavesi house [**Plates 56–58**] was built between 1913 and 1915 and should be remembered when you come to look at Hoffmann's buildings for the Werkbund exhibition in Cologne in 1914. The triangular pediments are quite specifically classical, though the mouldings are typically Hoffmann's own [**Plate 56**]. The vertical pilaster strips are treated with a sort of reeded surface which toys with the idea of classical fluting but shows that a more delicate effect is intended. In the central portion of this façade, the pilasters are wrapped round to form elliptical half-columns, carrying rather strange figurines in place of capitals [**Plate 58**]. On the garden side [**Plate 57**], we find the familiar cutting back of the mass of the building and the delicate contrast of rectilinear masses set off against intricate but reserved mouldings. Much of this vocabulary, particu-larly the floral motifs on the balustrade to the stairs, became the staple diet of Viennese designers and turns up again in slightly adapted motifs in the Art Deco style in Paris in the 1920s. A building like this helps to remind us how close to the surface classicism was among all the pupils of Otto Wagner and how narrow the boundary is between abstract purity of form and direct neoclassicism.

11 Adolf Loos (1870–1933)

Loos is the best known of the Viennese pioneers in inter-national terms, mainly because he lived and worked in France in the twenties when several of his writings were republished. Loos was born in 1870, the same year as Hoffmann, and he was taught building and architecture in several provincial schools. The years 1893–6 he spent in the USA, but we still know very little about his stay there, except that he mostly moved in German circles and that he saw the Chicago World's Fair in 1893. In 1896 he settled in Vienna to start an architectural career, but there are no designs before 1898. His main activity was journalism about fashion, design and architecture in newspapers and magazines from 1897 onwards. Read his article 'Archi-tecture' in *Form and Function* (no. 21). Although this was published quite late, it sums up ideas which he had been publishing since 1897. Read too, *Banham*, Chapter 7 and *Hitchcock*, pp. 472–6.

Loos was a keen admirer of Anglo-Saxon ways of life and design. Although he never talks about specific examples it seems that he derived his knowledge about English design from the journals and from the exhibitions in the Viennese Museum for Applied Arts. The sources for his ideas lie elsewhere. First of all his satirical style, which is new in architectural and design criticism, was strongly influenced by the writings of his friend Karl Kraus, the greatest Viennese satirist and journalist of the period. Loos was friendly with most *avant-garde* artists and musicians in Vienna: the painter Kokoschka, the composer Schœnberg and so forth. His writings contain deep moral convictions, of the kind the periodical *Der Kunstwart* and the writer Alfred Lichtwark propounded in Germany (cf. *Form and Function*, no. 6). Loos was associated with the Secession artists at first, but fell out with them very soon, in 1898 because, as it seems, Hoffmann did not let him design one of the interiors of the Secession building. He also thought that applying art to design was a mistake and ridiculed it in his articles, 'The Story of a Poor Rich Man' and 'Cultural Degeneration' (cf. *Form and Function*, no. 21). The basis of Loos's argument was again the *Zeitgeist*. Loos goes far beyond Wagner in discussing in detail those elements in which he already finds examples of 'modern life', especially the whole range of clothes; he writes articles about underwear, footwear, hats, suits, and the everyday crafts. The modern gentleman's suit is unobtrusive and appropriate, and the same fashion reigns in all civilized countries. The principle is to be 'well dressed' but not to be 'beautiful'. Dress has to do with *Kultur* (civilization, culture) not with art. Loos also discusses various kinds of special clothing, such as sports outfits. It is the functionality of these designs which attracts him. He praises cheap furniture, such as the simpler versions of the Thonet mass-produced bentwood chair. Here we find a chair, he says, which shows the specific way of sitting of a period without any disguise.

Two other writings after 1900 must be mentioned here: his most famous article, *Ornament und Verbrechen* (Ornament and Crime) first published in 1908, and *Architektur* (*Form and Function*, no. 21) of 1910. His message is again a very simple one: 'See that you express the time you belong to'. The sign of the modern period is in his view the lack of ornament: 'The evolution of civilization is identical with the eradication of ornament in objects of everyday use'. But as has often been pointed out, there are many contradictory arguments in his writings: on the one hand there is the emphasis on contemporaneity, on the other, he insists, like so many reformers in that period, on the validity of the 'anonymous' tradition, the tradition of craftsmanship, based on common sense. He also continually praises classical architecture, Greek, Roman

and Neoclassical. In most of the interiors he designed Loos preferred English eighteenth-century or *Biedermeier* furniture to contemporary designs. In many ways, Loos was a die-hard traditionalist. It is because he thought that the old standards were slipping that he was so vehement in attacking his contemporaries.

For the first ten years, Loos produced hardly anything but interior designs. What is remarkable is that Art Nouveau forms show themselves only very rarely. One of the earliest designs, the shop fittings for Goldmann and Salatsch of 1898, relies for its impact on rectilinear wooden framework. The showcases are fitted with small, square glass panes with chamfered edges, something that became characteristic of the mature Secession style. Loos himself puts the Café Museum of 1899 at the beginning of his career [**Plate 59**]. His work is confined to the interior and exterior of the ground floor of an ordinary corner block. The café consists of two spaces, opening into each other at right angles, one for billiards and the other for card games; in the centre is the circular stand for the cashier. The room on the whole looks very bare: one critic spoke of Loos's nihilism. There are rows of spindly metal lamps hanging down from the shallow vault (on the right in **Plate 59**).

Figure 32 Adolf Loos, Steiner House, Vienna, plan, 1910.

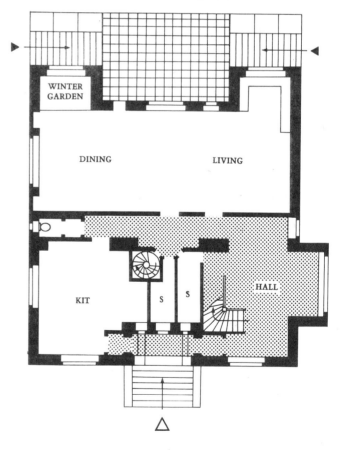

Figure 33   Adolf Loos, Steiner House, Vienna, 1910, street front.

There are the contrasts of the other materials, the heavy billiard tables in unvarnished mahogany set off against the metal parts. The chairs are a cheap Thonet bentwood model, after a special design by Loos.

During 1904–6 Loos altered and extended a villa at Montreux (Villa Karma) on Lake Geneva for a Viennese client [**Plate 60**]. He developed a typically Viennese liking for rich materials, marble, or precious heavy woods for wall surfaces and heavy wooden beams on the ceiling, or (as in **Plate 60**), metal sheets with exposed screws. All the forms and profiles are square, the surfaces smooth and polished. The effect, like that of the Palais Stoclet, depends on the sumptuousness of the materials and the clarity of the composition.

In 1910, he built his two most important pre-war buildings. The Steiner house [**Plate 61, Figs 32** and **33**] is a family dwelling in a Viennese suburb and has always been considered one of the first examples of the modern square box. It is an exceptional building in many ways: the plan is very simple and regular on two sides, hence the extreme regularity and symmetry of the street front and the garden front. The street front had to be as low as possible because Loos had to comply with rather archaic Viennese bye-laws. The side elevations, in contrast, show a highly irregular disposition of the openings and a profile

which shows how Loos squeezed in two more storeys than he was supposed to [**Plate 61**]. It is the plainness of the garden front that is always stressed. Indeed, the windows carry no decoration and there is nothing of Hoffmann's preciousness of detail. The flat roof of the garden front is echoed by the horizontal format of most of the windows— a subtler solution than Hoffmann's at the Purkersdorf Sanatorium [**Plates 36** and **37**]. There is no cornice (except for a thin layer of lead to protect the masonry), a rare phenomenon at the time, and there are only a few other examples in Loos's work. However, in an early article about Hoffmann's designs, Loos had already remarked that the latter rejected the cornice, at least in street architecture. What used to be called the Goldmann and Salatsch store at the Michaelerplatz in the centre of Vienna [**Plates 62** and **63**], like most of his shops, shows more ornamental detail. The ground floor and mezzanine are covered with marble but there are plain rendered walls with unornamented windows above. This signified that the apartments and flats above were to be used for different purposes from the shop below. The lower floors include correct Doric columns and entablature and some very Mackintosh-like small-paned oriel windows brought forward to the edge of the wall surface as on the south face of the Glasgow School of Art (cf. Units 3–4, Plate 73). Notice how subtle

Figure 34   Adolf Loos, competition entry for Chicago Tribune tower, 1922.

Loos is in his treatment of the scale of the different parts, If you follow the line of the lintel above the Doric columns. on the left [**Plate 63**], you will see how it crosses the oriel windows on the right in the form of a metal band. This level related to the big columns is directly contrasted to the small columns flanking the oriel windows. Walter Gropius learnt a lot from this building when he came to design the Fagus factory two years later. The interior was equally gaunt and symmetrical while adhering to simple geometric forms and relying on polished surfaces.

Loos's designs of the next decade are more difficult to understand. He very often resorted to classical vocabulary.

His contribution to the Chicago Tribune Competition not altogether flippantly consisted of a fluted Doric column, thirty-four storeys high [**Fig. 34**]. There is a tongue-in-cheek quality about this design, but it shows how Loos considered classicism to be the only monumental style.

Read the extracts by Loos in *Form and Function* (nos. 20 and 21). **How did he reconcile in practice his ideas of contemporaneity and traditionalism?**

● Since architecture and design have nothing to do with art, but are tools of civilization, just like a carriage or a man's suit, they have to derive their forms entirely from the particular purpose they are meant to serve and this can be linked to one particular moment in time and may change very rapidly. This concept was linked in a wider sense to the idea of the *Zeitgeist*, which means that in a given period all phenomena and all ideas are somehow linked and all can be explained from some central purpose. Nevertheless, Loos emphasizes the continuity of craftsmanship, which is not subject to fashion. Common sense is something that does not change every minute. The *bête noire* of all writers around 1900 was the second half of the nineteenth century with its rapidly changing stylistic phases. These, according to Loos, were not conditioned by real circumstances but were mere fashions, a pursuit after different schemes of decoration for the sake of variety. ●

Other theorists around 1900 avoided Loos's difficulty in that they did not strive for contemporaneity. The revivers of neoclassical architecture such as McKim, Mead and White, John Burnet and Geoffrey Scott in the Anglo-Saxon countries spoke of the continuity and the continuing validity of classical architecture. It had stood the test of time more than any other style, because it was based on simple—some would say common sense—concepts. Another group, the advocates of the vernacular revival, maintained that one should go back to simple rural architecture, also on the grounds of common sense. Paul Schultze-Naumburg, the architect and writer, condemned the nineteenth-century search for different styles as Loos did. He also rejected the contemporary enthusiasm for a new style, for *Jugendstil* in particular, which Loos also condemned, and even the search for a style which would express the new technologies (cf. 'Cultural Degeneration', by Loos, in *Form and Function*). In ordinary types of buildings such as houses, according to Schultze-Naumburg, the new elements of technology can be fitted quite easily into the traditional framework. Traditionalism versus Revivalism: this was the way most of the American, English and German neoclassical architects in the twentieth century wanted to distinguish themselves from the nineteenth century. In both his writings and his executed works, Loos fits into this context.

Part 4 Monumentality, Classicism and the architecture of pre-war Germany

1 Introduction

In 1890, a book appeared in Germany which proved popular so rapidly that it went into more than twenty editions in the first year of its publication: *Rembrandt als Erzieher* (Rembrandt the educator) anonymously written by 'a German'. It soon became known that Julius Langbehn (1851–1907) was the author, a strange person, who had studied many things and led an emotionally turbulent life without ever fitting into any ordinary profession. The book has no theme, its title is hardly very relevant, but it preaches certain views which were at that time devoured by most Germans who possessed a cultural background: German culture suffers from specialization and intellectualism, from academic exactitude, from foreign influence, from lack of individualism and lack of genius, etc. There is little specifically on the applied arts and architecture: Germany lacks a national architecture, there is too much preoccupation with detailed architectural history, there is a lack of monumentality and there should be large architectural monuments for events of national history. All these ideas had already been ventilated by architectural critics, yet the book was reviewed by architects, and as late as 1911, Hermann Muthesius referred to it as opening people's eyes about the importance of 'artistic culture versus scientific culture' (cf. *Form and Function*, no. 24).

One of the new themes that German architects were trying to develop was a new kind of monumentality. It can be said to have begun with the neo-Baroque in the 1880s. This had been the most recent stylistic fashion and it seemed to follow logically from the previous Renaissance revival, in that one could show how the growing wealth of the new German Empire (established in 1871) was expressed in more and more decoration and exuberance. But soon the Baroque came to be considered as more than just over-ornamentation: Heinrich Wölfflin (1864–1945) in his *Renaissance und Barock* of 1888, wrote that the principle of Baroque architecture is 'sublime massiveness', in which all parts are fused into one dynamic whole. Baroque architecture is overwhelming and overpowering and he compares its effect to the feeling conveyed in Richard Wagner's operas. The stylistic change from Renaissance to Baroque was not conditioned by techniques of construction, Wölfflin argues, but by a change in the feeling for form on the part of the artist. This attempt to minimize the importance of technical factors in architecture and to stress the formal and emotional elements becomes an important line of thought with many German architects in the following decades.

Wölfflin's views on the Baroque found their exact parallel in the activity of some young architects in the late 1880s in Berlin, who revived the eighteenth-century idea of architectural sketches, where they could defy both the practical and rational considerations of architecture, as well

as the demand for historical accuracy and detail. Their drawings showed vast buildings, simple massiveness contrasted with exuberant decoration, as well as complicated spatial arrangements. Of course, these exercises in the classical manner had one serious drawback, the lack of national feeling. Since the early nineteenth century, Gothic had been considered *the* German national style, but when one had to admit that it originated in France, its supporters were silenced, and also there was still some opposition to Gothic because of its Catholic associations. To many German architects from the 1880s onwards, the Romanesque seemed to fulfil the role of a national style; it was specifically thought of as an imperial style, dating from a time when the German emperors were still exercising strong rule; Kaiser Wilhelm II especially liked the idea. Yet the most decisive formal influence on the Romanesque revival in the 1890s came not from a national source at all, but from H. H. Richardson and his work in Boston, with its massive, clear geometrical forms and rugged surface. Very soon a building type emerged, which served as a vehicle for all these forms and ideas: the architectural monument.

The death of two Kaisers in one year, 1888, provided an opportunity for competitions and eventually for the erection of a large number of monuments [**Fig. 35**]. It was soon felt that the kind of monument that had been common in the previous decades, with its display of allegories and historical figures (such as the Albert Memorial in Kensington Gardens, London, of 1862) would not do any more. It had to be a building, simple, massive, planned in harmony with its surrounding landscape. As a critic summed up in 1907:

the effect of overpowering masses cannot be equalled by any other art form; the deepest feelings, the deepest reverence, the deepest grief of death . . . national feeling . . . power and greatness of personality . . . to be expressed in the abstract language of harmonies.

(F. Schumacher, *Streifzuge eines Architekten*, Jena, 1920, p. 110)

Figure 35   G. Halmhuber, Architectural Fantasy, 1888.

Figure 36   B. Schmitz, Kyffhäuser Monument, 1891–6.   *Figure 37   W. Kreis, Bismarck Monument project, 1899.*

The most prolific designer of such monuments in the 1890s was Bruno Schmitz (1858–1916), whose monuments near Koblenz, Minden and on the Kyffhäuser Mountains in Thuringia are still there. He began designing this kind of building in the 1880s, at first in the classical mode, but a visit to the USA convinced him of the superioirity of Richardson's Romanesque, and he combined the heavy overall rustication with a kind of castellated medievalizing style [**Fig. 36**].

2   Wilhelm Kreis (1813–1955)

The most important designer in this context was Wilhelm Kreis. He became widely known when he won the competition for the *Völkerschlachtdenkmal* (People's battle monument) at Leipzig in 1897, at the age of twenty-four. The commission which was to celebrate the victory over Napoleon at Leipzig in 1813, subsequently went to Bruno Schmitz and it became the largest of all German monuments completed in 1913. But Kreis's most influential designs came in 1899, when he won the first three prizes for the competition for a monument to Bismarck [**Fig. 37**].

Bismarck's fame, especially after his death in 1899, eclipsed that of the old Kaiser, Wilhelm I, and it was he who was considered the symbol of the new German power. Nationalistically minded German student associations decided to build monuments in all German university towns and, moreover, 'on all prominent hills in Germany' —about fifty of them were built in all. Because of the relatively small size of the Bismarck monument, about forty feet high, it had to be as simple and massive as possible, in order to impress from a distance. On a square base there are four heavy columns which form part of a larger mass, filling the space between them. There are slightly more detailed forms at the cornice, which is crowned by a kind of attic. But the contour remains smooth and the surfaces consist of roughly hewn, dark masonry. The only more figurative element is an abstract German eagle, almost merged with the structure. The mottoes Kreis chose for his three entries came from Richard Wagner's operas and Beethoven's music: 'Götter-dämmerung', 'Wotan' and 'Eroica'. Most of the other designs for the competition chose geometric or other simplified forms; only a minority adhered to figurative solutions, such as an armoured fist or half a knight in armour (the 'Iron Chancellor').

Kreis does not usually figure among the pioneers of the Modern Movement. The reasons are clear. He always preferred highly monumental commissions, and his last patrons were the Nazis, and there is little change as far as the formal concepts are concerned. But his early designs remain an important chapter in the development of abstract architectural forms. As far as the political content is concerned, one cannot distinguish between respectable and non-respectable architects before World War I. One has to be reminded that even Mies van der Rohe entered a competition for a Bismarck monument over the Rhine in 1912. **What do you suppose was the importance of this interest in the 'new monumentality' for modern architecture?**

● Monumentality in architecture is something that is only vaguely defined. Each period has a different view of what kind of architecture was particularly monumental. The more traditional use of the term 'monumental architecture' refers to certain types of buildings rather than a certain style: it means large, public buildings in contrast to simpler, private ones. For the classical style this would mean the full use of the repertoire of classical forms, such as a portico, or giant pilasters, etc. The new monumentality however, means first of all simple forms. These simple forms must be associated with size, if not a large size in reality, then a large size in appearance, in contrast to its setting. This is something that can often better be shown when the architect presents his design in a drawing, rather than when one stands in front of the building. Since Piranesi's fantastic sketches of Roman architectures in the eighteenth century, architects and architectural draughts-men have tried to inflate the size and importance of their buildings in their sketches and perspectives. Another reason for simplicity is the integration of the building or architectural monument into the landscape. Also, when seen from afar, inscriptions or figurative detail could not be read and would not make sense. Thus it is claimed that the symbolism of a building, particularly if it is a monu-ment (or a crematorium), can best be conveyed by simple, massive forms and by size. The theory that lies behind this is that when we look at a building, we associate its structure, whether for instance it is light or heavy, with our bodily functions, or gravitational behaviour. Thus, a heavy building can make us feel oppressed or impressed. This was part of the aesthetic theory of 'empathy', which was discussed by many philosophers and critics in those years. Another reason for choosing simple and massive, even clumsy forms, was the interest in archaic, primitive cultures, in which purity and honesty had not yet been corrupted by modern civilization. And in Germany the concept of the primitive or the archaic was combined with national political and cultural, and later, racial ideologies.

Thus the continuation of this kind of style in the years 1933–45 under the Nazis is not surprising. ●

3 Peter Behrens

In Behrens's work of 1900–2, we saw a strong tendency towards rigid patterning combined with voluptuous curves. During the years 1902–4, Behrens completely abandoned *Jugendstil* curves. In 1903 he became Director of the School of Applied Arts at Düsseldorf where he came under the influence of J. L. M. Lauweriks (1874–1932), a Dutchman who was then teaching at the Düsseldorf School. Lauweriks had worked with Dutch Gothicists and studied Gothic laws of proportion, also under the influence of Viollet-le-Duc's writings. He joined the Theosophical Society, a body concerned among other things, with the mystical sig-nificance of simple geometric shapes and pure colours—and which had a strong influence on artists and movements of the next decade, notably the painter Wassily Kandinsky and the *De Stijl* group. Berlage had used proportional systems in the design for his Amsterdam Exchange, and one of his interiors, the Chamber of Commerce, com-pleted before 1903, actually showed a rectangular decora-tive surface patterning reminiscent of Behrens's work. Nobody, however, in those years, made use of geometric shapes as decorative patterns to the extent that Behrens did (film strip frame 12). Apart from a number of domestic commissions Behrens was mainly designing exhibition buildings [**Figs. 38–41**] including gardens, exhibition restaurants and pergolas. The curved contours are now replaced by square ones, most buildings and larger pieces of furniture consisting of a series of squares added to each other or projecting into each other. The curved ornaments are replaced by straight lines and squares. Some of the interiors of the exhibition buildings at Mannheim and Dresden [**Fig. 40**] are covered with a veneer of carefully rendered and lively coloured surfaces, framed by carefully drawn black lines. Behrens wanted to show 'pure Euclidean geometry'. During the years 1906–11, Behrens was allowed to present some examples of this style at Hagen (Westphalia), under the patronage of the industrialist, Karl Ernst Osthaus. The first was the crematorium of 1906–7, which virtually repeats the decorative patterns of the Cologne exhibition. In his Villa Cuno [**Plate 64**] of 1908–11, and the Villa Schröder (*Hitchcock*, Fig. 277), begun in 1909, he abandons his geometric surface decoration, at least on the outside. The main characteristic of these houses is the extreme degree of symmetry and the geometrical classical features, especially the strong cornice line. In the AEG pavilion [**Fig. 41**], at the Berlin Shipbuilding Exhibition of 1908, the bulk of the building and the geometry of the whole is much emphasized.

Figure 38   Peter Behrens, Oldenburg Exhibition buildings, 1905.

Figure 39   Peter Behrens, temporary garden pergolas in the German Shipbuilding Exhibition, 1908.

Figure 40   Peter Behrens, Third German Kunstgewerbe Exhibition in Dresden, 1906, music room.

An earlier building, Haus Schede, in the Ruhr [**Fig. 42**], shows how Behrens could combine part of his curvilinear aesthetic with a highly sophisticated geometric organization. If you look carefully at this illustration, you will see how every detail is worked into the framework of a circle inscribed in a square. The very open treatment of the window is also notable. However austere the exteriors of his houses became, his interiors always retained a sense of warmth and human scale.

Behrens's contribution to office and factory design will be discussed in a later section. Of his other designs before 1914, only one can be mentioned here, his German Embassy in Petrograd[1] [**Fig. 43**], completed just before the war. In many of his works Behrens came close to Neoclassical design. The Embassy uses Doric columns and a cornice, Renaissance keystones, rustication and so forth. But none of these motifs is used in a strictly classical way. The proportion of the column is too elongated, the interval is too narrow, in order to create a more vertical effect to

Figure 41   Peter Behrens, A.E.G. Pavilion at the German Shipbuilding Exhibition, 1908.

Figure 42   Peter Behrens, Haus Schede, c. 1906, living room.

[1] Now Leningrad.

Figure 43 Peter Behrens, German Embassy, Petrograd (now Leningrad), 1911–12, elevation perspective drawing.

counteract the long, low shape of the building. The rustication is not very rough, but then the surface of the column is not very smooth. There is a subtle contrast between power and massiveness and elegant proportions.

By 1910, many German architects insisted on classical regularity and systems of proportion, seldom, however, on a faithful use of classical decorative detail. The Karlsruhe theorist, Friedrich Ostendorf, published some influential books on architectural theory, in which his main message was to disregard the picturesque and to avoid variations in planning: the exterior of a building should be a regular geometric form.

4 Troost, Schultze-Naumburg and Tessenow

During the late 1890s, when almost everybody in Munich joined the Art Nouveau bandwagon, a few designers tried something else. Franz Stuck (1863–1898), another painter of the Munich Secession group designed a lavish villa for himself in 1897 [**Plate 65**]. He developed a world of astringent Greek fantasy in the interior, with statues, reliefs and paintings, embedded in lavish patterns of decoration, where, however, geometrically arranged lines predominate, probably due to the influence of early Greek vase designs. Two years later another remarkable, classically designed interior appeared, the Heymel apartment, mentioned and illustrated in *Pevsner*, Fig. 131. Here it was not so much Greek decoration, but Neoclassical (or 'Empire', as the French and Germans call it) furniture with square outlines and polished wood surfaces that dominated the effect. The architect who assisted R. A. Schröder with the Heymel apartment was the young Paul Ludwig Troost (1878–1934). During 1903–4, Troost began a remarkable villa for the painter Benno Becker in Munich. While the plan is rather irregular, there is an intense symmetry on the exterior, especially at the entrance front, with a Baroque central projecting bar and portico. The most interesting part is the garden front with its carefully balanced asymmetry, its carefully proportioned windows which carry no

decoration and the isolated, but direct citations from Neoclassicism, Ionic and Doric columns. Art Nouveau forms are completely lacking and replaced by geometry, probably influenced by Vienna, and neoclassicism. Troost's further work is of little significance otherwise, but it must be mentioned that he became one of Hitler's favourite architects in the early years of the Third Reich. His most famous building is the *Haus der Deutschen Kunst* (German Art House), the art exhibition building in the Prinz-regentenstrasse in Munich, which in its simplified classicism can be seen as a continuation of the tendencies after 1900. The point of including these Neoclassical designs is to show that architects arrived at a pure, austere simplicity from different sources.

Another architect who followed the course of geometrical abstraction was Heinrich Tessenow. His main concern was the simple house, and his roots were in the vernacular revival. He had for some time been assistant to Paul Schultze-Naumburg (1869–1949) who was the chief writer on questions of vernacular architecture and on the preservation of the countryside and villages. It is significant that even in this field we find a turn against the picturesque. For Schultze-Naumburg, German peasant cottages [**Fig. 44**] are remarkable precisely because they are not just picturesque, but because they serve as models for a simple type of architecture, a simple rectangle with a large, dominating roof. In his houses for Hellerau Garden City near Dresden [**Plate 66**] Tessenow further geometrized these simple peasant-type houses and also tended to build all his houses in one row exactly alike. In his hands, the vernacular types acquired an almost machine-like uniformity, no longer picturesque. The small gabled design remained the most popular type for the German suburban house almost to the present day. For larger houses, Schultze-Naumburg recommended a revival of *Biedermeier*, the German vernacular Neoclassicism. It is as difficult to try to identify the precise historical precedents for this revival, as it is easy to see the formal and moral implications: simplicity and regularity.

Figure 44 Paul Schultze-Naumburg, workers' houses.

The most curious building of this whole group is perhaps the Assembly House and Theatre that Heinrich Tessenow built in the centre of Hellerau around 1910 [**Plate 67**]. It combines elements of the greatest formality, like the central portico, with such informal, almost cottage-like elements as small dormer windows on the roofs of the side wings flanking that same portico. The classical features of the portico, are again, far from usual or 'correct': they have square piers, placed unusually close to each other; the only indication of a capital is a small incised line.

Following on from what we had to report about Troost's later career it has to be mentioned that Schultze-Naumburg was to become Hitler's chief adviser in housing, where he continued to propagate his simple German house type, which he considered common sense—in contrast to what he called the extravaganzas of the International Style. As for Tessenow, no direct involvement with the Nazi regime is known, but he was influential as a teacher of Hitler's second favourite architect, Albert Speer.

Part 5　The Beaux-Arts tradition in France and the new materials

1　Introduction

The main developments in France in our period have been intensively dealt with by several writers: Banham in the first chapters of *Theory and Design in the First Machine Age* (set book), Peter Collins on the problems of concrete in his book *Concrete, The Vision of a New Architecture* (recommended reading), and L. Hautecoeur with the developments before 1900 in the last volume (VII) of his *Histoire de l'architecture classique en France* (Paris, 1857). Professor Collins will be covering this subject matter more thoroughly in Radio Programme 6 (RV). Read *Pevsner* pages 179–81 and *Banham*, pages 36–42. If you have time, read pages 178–86 of the book by Peter Collins. **What are the chief characteristics of French architecture to which these authors draw attention?**

● All three authors stress the importance of the technical innovations in the work of the architects they select, but they differ widely as to the relationship between technical advances and aesthetic considerations. The way Pevsner sees it is that new materials are used and shown to be used (especially concrete in Perret's case) in defiance of traditional laws of form and decoration. Banham wants to reduce the element of technical innovation and stress the formal elements. For Collins, the formal and traditional classical element that he sees very strongly in Perret's work, seems to be laudable and not a retrograde step. ●

How are we to evaluate these differing opinions? We can say that they seem to be in line with the differences which have persisted among architectural historians writing about our period (they are certainly strongly felt in the literature about the architecture dealt with further on). Ultimately, these differences of outlook go back to the period itself and its background. A brief outline of the currents in French architectural thinking in the later nineteenth century might therefore be of some help. One has to begin with the fact that in France in that period we observe considerably more progress in all kinds of engineering architecture than in most other major countries, especially England. Although most of the work was done by designers who called themselves engineers and who in most cases employed 'architects' as designers for added decorations, there was a large body of opinion among architects and critics who regarded iron, steel and soon concrete as essential elements, not only for engineering, but for architecture as a whole, capable of providing answers to that biting question of the nineteenth century, the question of a new style. This trend of architectural thinking was called the Rationalist school. As far as the historical starting point for a new departure was concerned, most of the writers firmly believed in the Gothic style and the

main protagonists of the Gothicists was E. E. Viollet-le-Duc (cf. also Units 3–4, p. 47). For Viollet-le-Duc, good architecture was rational construction, with all decoration closely related to construction; and thirteenth-century Gothic was the most perfect embodiment of this kind of architecture. As a tribute to the nineteenth century, he pleaded for the use of iron in certain parts of the building, while still maintaining that on the whole, pure iron constructions, such as Les Halles in Paris, could only be considered as 'engineering'. Viollet-le-Duc's influence on the period around 1900, on Horta and Berlage, has already been discussed in Units 3–4.

On the other hand the tradition of classical architecture, with its stress on simple repetitive forms, on symmetry, proportional laws and order, had always been strong in France. Furthermore, these formal elements were initially not seen as opposing rational constructional values in architecture. The French classical school traditionally maintained that the basic classical elements, column and architrave, post and lintel, could also be seen as the most rational elements in architecture. It was the Gothic school that condemned classical architecture as mere decoration, as sham, concealing true construction. But since the 1870s, some architects, especially at the Ecole des Beaux-Arts—which also contained the main teaching institution in French architecture—began to challenge the theoretical supremacy of the Gothic Rationalists. They wanted to stress the formal elements, the appeal to the senses, not just the fulfilment of a practical function, and they considered the long tradition of classical architecture—without advocating firmly any of its historical varieties—as a way out of the nineteenth-century historicist fashions. Construction and function should be put into a secondary place after proportion, decoration and external values. As a result, a stricter and grander classical vocabulary and layout came back into public and commercial architecture and the most exuberant decorations seemed permissible, e.g. at the Paris International Exhibition of 1900 (cf. Units 3–4, Figs. 5–9). It parallels the return to the 'Grand Manner' in England and America. In the broadest terms, the development of the work and thinking of those architects in France who have been selected for the histories of the Modern Movement, represent a continuation of the tendencies outlined above and perhaps a solution of the dilemma.

Let us, then, briefly sketch the writings and buildings of the protagonists. We could start with an example of what one could call 'practical' Rationalism. François Hennebique perfected reinforced concrete in the 1890s, and he was concerned with the engineering aspects of countless buildings in that material. When he built his own office at 1 rue Danton in 1898 of reinforced concrete, he achieved great fame with the way he made maximum use of a very narrow site, by reducing the thickness of the walls. Yet, in a manner typical of the later nineteenth century, he employed an architect to devise decorations for the façade in the eclectic style used for medium-status street architecture at the time.

Anatole de Baudot (1834–1915), in contrast, was an architect and restorer and one of the closest followers of Viollet-le-Duc. He shared the belief of the Rationalist thinkers that the new materials should be made use of in the search for a new architectural expression. In his best known building, St Jean de Montmartre [**Plates 68** and **69**], 1897, he made use of concrete, but he did not contribute to technical developments. In fact, he used a slightly old-fashioned system, that of reinforced cement, which made use of a lot of brick as reinforcement. He was equally convinced that the Gothic system of vaulting should still remain the basis of modern architecture and thus he designed a rib-vaulted building with intersecting arches. The formal novelties lie more in the details [**Plate 69**] and handling, such as the lack of capitals or any other horizontal divisions in the framework, and the crispness and precision with which the different ribs are fitted together. The walls are treated as pure planes, with the arches cut out of them with no mouldings at all. Notice how some of the spandrels are glazed where you would least expect it and how thin the supports are.

Banham introduces the writings of two theorists at the beginning of his account, J. Guadet (1834–1908), *Eléments et théories de l'architecture* (Paris, 1902) and A. Choisy (1841–1905), *Histoire de l'architecture* (Paris, 1899). Again, we find a summing up and a combination of our problems. Both books share a strong element of Rationalism. But Guadet also stresses the 'art' of architecture, not just construction, and the most important aspect of the architect's work is composition, the putting together of the individual parts conditioned by function and construction. Indeed, the exercises of the pupils at the Ecole des Beaux-Arts, where Guadet taught, mostly consisted of the simple axial and orderly organization on paper of large projects. Guadet did not want to prescribe any precise versions of classical architecture, nor any other historical style, but understood classical as a general sense of order and beauty.

For Choisy, Viollet-le-Duc's heritage was much stronger. The overriding explanation of the course of architectural history was the development of structural innovations. Yet Choisy always seeks the simplest and most direct structural solution, whether Greek temples or Gothic churches, and this is underlined by his extremely neat and poignant drawing style (see *Banham*, Figs. 6–8).

Tony Garnier (1869–1948) and Auguste Perret (1874–1954) both came out of the Ecole des Beaux-Arts in the 1890s. Both were imbued with the doctrines of Guadet and Choisy and both continued and modified the French tradition in the way these authors had done. Garnier's main contribution was in the field of town planning, his project for a *Cité Industrielle* (1904–17) was the best known early project with completely worked out zoning and a radically new approach to a wide range of urban problems. This will be discussed in Radio Programme 5 (RV). Many of the buildings he outlined in his project were to be built in reinforced concrete, but he rarely mentions matters of construction in his comments. Thus his main contribution seems a visual one, that of geometric simplicity and almost total abstraction from classical detail. In some of his public buildings, such as the Heliotherapeutic Institute and some of his houses he even dispenses with cornices, leaving a completely bare cube.

2 Auguste Perret (1874–1954)

The works of Perret that are of importance here, are three buildings in Paris: his apartment block, 25 bis rue Franklin, of 1903 [**Fig. 45** and Radiovision booklet, Programme 6, Figs. 6 and 7] the Garage Ponthieu of 1905 (*Hitchcock*, Fig. 256) and the Théâtre des Champs Elysées of 1911 (*Banham*, Fig. 14). All these buildings exploit the constructional possibilities of reinforced concrete. In the apartment block he uses this concrete mainly to gain greater openness of plan [**Fig. 45**] and larger windows on a restricted site, but hardly has to bridge spans that could not have been dealt with by using conventional materials. The concrete framework is covered, partly for practical reasons, with tiles. These tiles, however, follow very closely the contours of the framework, and on the whole the building in its angularity stands in marked contrast to Art Nouveau curved smoothness, or post-Art Nouveau solidity. Perret himself called the Garage Ponthieu the 'première tentative

Figure 45 Auguste Perret, apartment block, 25 bis rue Franklin, Paris, plan, top floor.

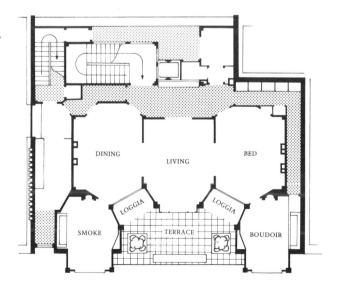

(au monde) du béton armé esthétique' (the world's first experiment in aesthetic reinforced concrete). From the constructional point of view it is certainly true that the large spans and the thin supports of the framework, which is not covered by anything, could not be constructed in conventional materials. But both Collins and Banham stress the formal aspects more: the careful spacing of the intervals, the centre one being wider than the side, the spacing and proportioning of the other, minor supports; the way the upper storey is reminiscent of an attic; and the two cylindrical, non-constructional supports in the main entrance derived from classical porticos. For the Théâtre des Champs Elysées, Perret was initially called in as an engineer (Van de Velde, who first designed the building, had been unable to solve those problems). Again, in Perret's final design there is a contrast between the ingeniously thin framework of the building, and the heavy walls and piers of the façades.

Thus the French architects and critics seem to have been, on the one hand, intensively concerned with developing or using new methods of construction; on the other, they used systems of proportioning and ordering that can only be called purely formal. Banham makes a crucial remark in his discussion of Choisy's writings—and Collins would no doubt agree with it: '. . . as a Rationalist [Choisy] is naturally inclined toward the orderly and logical. . . .'[1] Seen in this light, there does not seem such a dichotomy after all.

[1] Banham, set book, p. 28.

Part 6 Industry, the Werkbund and German design for the machine

1 Introduction

In this chapter, many of the ideas occurring earlier in these units are developed and begin to take on a different slant. As in so many situations throughout history, it is the economic situation that spurs on design awareness. Partly because of this, some designers in Germany became aware of the need to design for machine-made, mass-produced objects. Through the influence of England and the interest in simply expressed forms and good quality craftsmanship, the standard and the awareness of design was fairly high by 1905. But you must remember how this had been achieved, for it is in this that we can find the reason for some of the contradictions in design in Germany from 1907–14. This awareness had been achieved by an emphasis on good quality craftsmanship, the use of simple forms, and the involvement of people originally trained as artists, in designing. In most cases these aspects formed a hindrance to the development of design for machinery and mass production. At the end of this chapter you will see how most designers in Germany in 1914 were still dubious about standardization in design, and likewise were beginning to depart from the use of simple geometric forms and take up more expressive ones. There was a lively debate on these issues throughout the pre-war period, however, and you can dip into it in the extracts printed in *Form and Function* (especially nos. 19, 23 and 24) and *Documents*, nos. 1.1–1.4.

2 New developments in German industrial architecture

German commercial and industrial architecture in many ways repeats the story of the Chicago School in the 1880s, and 1890s (which will be covered in Units 7–8) and parallels the French developments: there was an acceptance of a new type of building into the realm of respectable, even 'monumental' architecture, not by adding a conventional classical or Gothic façade, but by emphasizing certain functional and constructional aspects and by stressing the formal concepts of simple outline and massive walls. Read *Banham*, Chapter 6.

The interest of active and forward-looking architects in Europe around 1900 was not on the whole concentrated on industrial architecture, but on the house and its interior fittings. In Vienna, Wagner and his school, with their greater stress on 'Modern Life', made a point of including office buildings and modern constructions in their work. But most of the architects who designed the apartment blocks, offices and department stores in the new cities were unadventurous as architects, despite innovations in construction, planning and services. In Germany, too, it was in the context of urban architecture, in the work of architects who worked on a variety of urban commissions,

that the importance of new building types emerged. The outstanding example is the Wertheim department store in Berlin [**Plates 70–72**], begun in 1897 and completed in 1904. The architect, Adolf Messel, was one of the busiest and most respected figures in Berlin in those years. He was an eclectic in the sense that he refused to take part in any of the puristic style movements of the day. He happily continued to use and mix Gothic, Baroque, and Neo-classical, but cleverly and sensitively adapted each mode to the problem in hand. There are several novel features in the Wertheim store. The first section of the building is in iron and glass and extremely functional, if rather bare [**Plate 70**]. The later part of the exterior towards Leipzigerstrasse [**Plate 71**] consists of a series of vertical supports alternating with rows of long thin windows over wide arches on the ground floor. There is a lot of decoration but it is small in scale and appears subordinate to the whole structure. The roof is large, rather domestic looking, with its quiet surfaces and horizontality in complete contrast to the façade. In terms of styles the building is a hybrid mixture, dominated by a kind of 'Gothic verticality'. It was the later part which was considered more 'architectural' and illustrated everywhere. The interior was perhaps more remarkable, in that it was completely open plan [**Plate 72**] not only with large stair halls, as was indeed customary in department stores, but so that one could see through all the floors from one end of the building to the other, thus letting in as much daylight as possible. The combination of the steel structure and its open interior with the dignified and 'architectural' façade impressed most German critics. Carl Scheffler, Berlin's foremost architectural critic emphasized the new dignity of commercial architecture: the 'petty traders look' had been replaced by something 'monumental' and many people were hoping for a 'renewal of the whole of architecture' following the example of the Wertheim department store.[1] The most important surviving store of this kind is Olbrich's Kaufhof (formerly Warenhaus Tietz) in Düsseldorf 1906–8 [**Plates 73** and **74**]. It is worth comparing them closely. The main difference is that Olbrich dresses up his interior more than Messel did, with a lot of marble surfaces. But his design is also more clean and simple in its impact. There was a considerable amount of exposed iron inside Messel's store and it was only slightly decorated. The use of iron in 'architecture' (as opposed to in buildings which were mere engineering), had been considered a problem not only in a technical sense, but also in an aesthetic sense, since the middle of the nineteenth century. The arguments are summarized in *Documents*, no. 5.3 and *Form and Function*, nos. 16, 26 and 57. From the 1890s onwards, many iron buildings, such as the shed of the Central Station in Hamburg of 1901, managed to create firmer outlines and to achieve a certain air of solidity through rigid repetition of forms and through leaving out decorative details. Also,

[1] Carl Scheffler, *Moderne Baukunst*, Berlin, 1907, p. 46.

Art Nouveau as practised by Victor Horta and Hector Guimard had taught people to see aesthetic virtue in purely linear and delicate arrangements of curves. It was precisely these visual qualities that the art historian A. G. Meyer alluded to in his book of 1907, *Eisenbauten: ihre Geschichte und Aesthetik* (Iron architecture, its history and aesthetics).[1] It is essential to note that Meyer insists that he is not advocating pure engineering architecture, that is, the recognition of any construction as aesthetically viable. Like most German critics as well as his French contemporaries, and in contrast to Wagner, he maintains that a new style cannot simply spring from construction but must be derived from a feeling for form. However, at the end he admits, somewhat meekly, that the new iron aesthetic might also arrive at forms dictated by construction through a general process of acclimatization. These ideas are repeated throughout the writings of the foremost German architects in this field, Muthesius, Behrens and Gropius. A new monumental style for modern types of buildings and modern construction cannot be brought about by attaching decorations in the manner of the nineteenth century, nor by simply declaring engineering 'architecture', but by somehow making engineering more monumental and by combining it with monumental stone architecture.

How the industrial architecture of Behrens and Gropius fits into this pattern will become clear in the next section. The third architect who must be mentioned here is Hans Poelzig, active mainly in Breslau in Silesia. Poelzig had a number of industrial commissions before 1914. One of the most interesting was the unbuilt project for a mill and warehouse (Werdermühle, Breslau) of 1906 [**Fig. 46**]. It is in brick, with very massive, simple outlines. The only

decoratively treated features are the windows, all of them with the same semicircular head, and the rounded corners of the building. The chemical factory at Luban [**Plate 75** and *Banham*, p. 59] is similarly treated with its large surfaces of sheer brick interrupted by square- and round-headed windows. Poelzig made less use of iron, at least externally[2], but his water tower-cum-exhibition building at Posen of 1911 (*Banham*, p. 59) is a kind of half-timbering in iron with brick infilling. The interior [**Plate 76**] has a flavour of machine romanticism in its massive use of iron. This was not just a utilitarian building. There was a restaurant and an exhibition area. Of the many experiments with reinforced concrete, only one can be mentioned here: Max Berg's *Jahrhunderthalle* (Centenary Hall) in Breslau [**Plates 77–79**], a vast space, covered by a network of reinforced concrete arches. Interestingly, the exterior of this building tells little of the curves: it appears as a series of vertical strips of windows, and the main entrance is treated as a portico with thinned-out concrete classical columns. One is reminded of Behrens, who said that the best expression of basic constructional elements was not a construction in modern materials but the classic Greek temple. Max Berg's Centenary Hall is really a reinforced concrete adaptation of one of the great Byzantine churches, like the Hagia Sophia in Constantinople. This is especially clear in the plan [**Fig. 47**]. The system of stepped back windows in the dome, however, came from industrial architecture.

Figure 47   Max Berg, Jahrhunderthalle in Breslau, 1913.

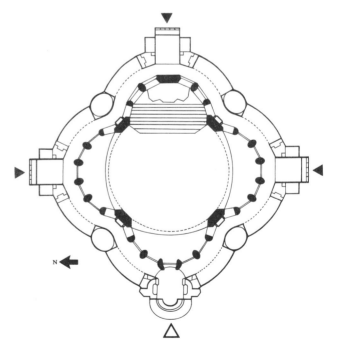

Figure 46   Hans Poelzig Watermill Project, Breslau 1906.

[1] A. G. Meyer, *Eisenbauten: ihre Geschichte und Aesthetik*, Esslingen, 1907.

[2] Note, however, the steel and glass wall on the flank of the watermill project, **Fig. 46**.

3   Behrens and the AEG factories

The television programme for these two weeks consists of a comparison between the work of Behrens and Gropius at the AEG and Fagus shoe-last factories respectively. Some of the background information for these prestigious industrial commissions needs to be explained here. AEG, under Emil Rathenau, had always employed top architects as designers for their factories and even their industrial products, as had most of the big competitive firms in the new industries of electrical generation and small motor manufacture, such as Siemens. Franz Schwechten, Adolf Messel and Otto Eckmann had worked for AEG before Behrens. The interest and publicity given to the construction of these huge factories was at least partly due to the novelty of the industry and the actual scale of the undertakings which AEG was contemplating. When the Turbine factory was built, in 1908–9 [**Plates 80, 81** and *Hitchcock,* Fig. 278], it was probably the biggest shed in existence in Berlin, if you consider the enclosed volume of the main space. Most factory buildings at the time consisted of lower, wider and more dispersed spaces, lined with rows

of cast-iron columns which carried simple, lightweight roofs with more or less adequate ventilation and lighting. AEG had had just such a machine hall on its Brunnenstrasse site since 1895, but the difficulty was that the overhead gantries had such a limited clearance and relied on such a shaky framework that moving very large and heavy pieces around the factory floor was extremely difficult. A path had to be cleared right through all the other industrial activities to run any large components out via the railway track, which served each aisle of the shed, and this led to intolerable wasted effort. The basic concept behind the Turbine factory on the Huttenstrasse site was that all the major component parts of the vast generators and turbines could be moved at will along the length of the shed and be served by any of the pieces of plant (lathe, drill, cable winder and so forth) in any order. So the building is constructed round a huge and massive gantry which is high enough off the ground to lift any loads clear of obstructions caused by the machinery, but not so high that it infringed Berlin planning regulations for street frontage height [**Fig. 48**]. The engineer in charge, Karl Bernhardt, was generally considered to be the best industrial

Figure 48   Peter Behrens, A.E.G. Turbine Factory, Berlin, 1908–9.

(a) Section

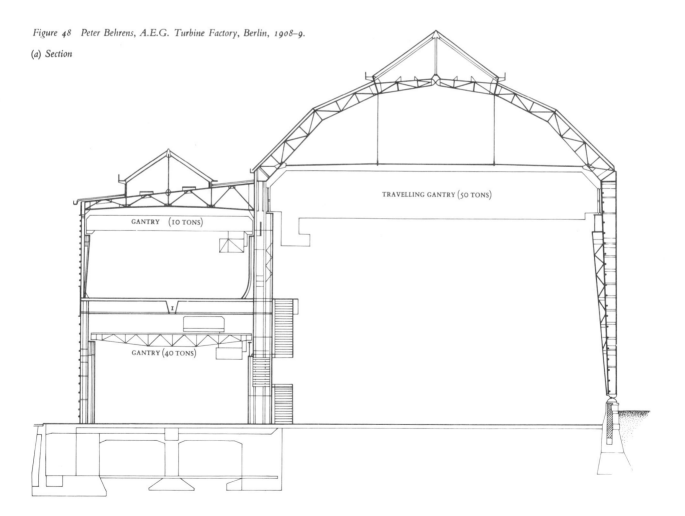

GANTRY (10 TONS)

TRAVELLING GANTRY (50 TONS)

GANTRY (40 TONS)

Figure 48   (b) Plan

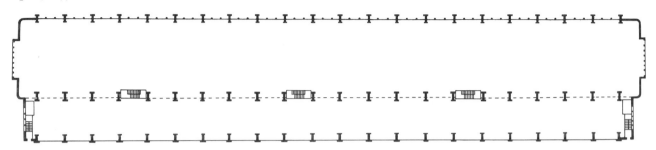

engineer of the time. He worked on many other huge undertakings, including an excellent factory in collaboration with Hermann Muthesius. In **Plate 80,** you can see the scale of the operations in the Turbine Hall and the clearance allowed to the gantry. Notice how the gantry rails are supported by additional girders bolted on to the main supports but not continued above. Now read the descriptions of the building given in *Documents* (nos. 5.1 and 5.2). Notice particularly how much emphasis Karl Bernhardt puts on the aesthetic factors in the design contributed by Behrens. The key point is that the actual form of the structure is conceived in such a way that there is an aesthetic value to be derived from every part of it. Some of these points are made specifically in the television programme. Notice, though, how the concrete corners of the building [**Plate 81**], look much less like masonry, and more like a thin screen of infill the closer you get. The frame of the main window in the end of the building is of massive proportions and a genuine supporting member, while the concrete skin is cut away with inset metal bands which echo the main horizontal glazing bars in the window.

The main AEG site, which Rathenau acquired piece by piece during the twenty years before the First World War, was situated between the Brunnenstrasse, Voltastrasse and the Hussitenstrasse [**Fig. 49**], in one of the industrial suburbs of Berlin, not far from the Huttenstrasse site. By the turn of the century, there was already intense productive activity on the site, with six or seven factory buildings operational. One of the more sober brick buildings by Johann Kraaz can be seen in **Plate 82.** Despite a basically utilitarian approach based on large steel windows, Kraaz's building still shows the need for fiddly strips of brick for articulation, in the style derived from Messel. Behrens's water tower betrays a direct influence from Olbrich's Wedding Tower, Darmstadt [**Plate 46**]. The plot had a complex railway siding, with permanent track installed more or less as it is today (dashed lines on the plan, **Fig. 49**). The plan of these tracks, curving in from the north west corner of the site, dictated the overall form of the High Tension factory, which was one of the earlier buildings Behrens designed on this site. Like the Turbine factory,

the main change compared to the older industrial buildings, as far as planning and arrangement were concerned, was that the new High Tension factory was much taller, rising to five storeys in the workshop wings, which surrounded the two central assembly sheds. If you look at **Plate 83**, you can see the very clear differentiation of the side blocks from the central, single-storey sheds. Compare this view with **Plate 84**, one of the preparatory sketches for the High Tension factory by Bernhardt and Behrens. Notice the fact that in the drawing, which remained the official scheme long after construction had started on the southern range of the building, the diagonal staircase windows in both of the towers which form the ends to the workshop wings, are symmetrically arranged. When Behrens came to supervise the construction of the last part of the building, towards the end of 1910, however, he decided to change this symmetrical arrangement somewhat, moving the

Figure 49   A.E.G. Factories on the Brunnenstrasse site, Berlin.

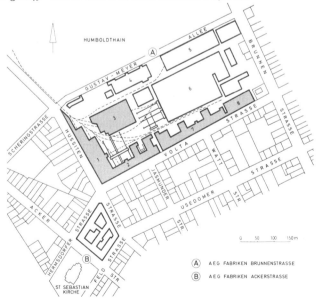

(1) *Assembly Hall (1911–12) (South end not finished till 1925)* (2) *Railway material factory (1911–13)* (3) *High Tension factory (1909–1910)* (7) *Small motors factory (1909–1913)* (8) *Later extension to small motors factory.*

staircase windows onto the side of the tower [**Plate 83**]. This point seems to me quite important in that it shows how pragmatic Behrens was and how seriously he took the rationalist concept of revealing on the outside what the internal functions of the building were. Another example of a similar last minute change of mind can be seen in the Assembly Hall [**Plate 85**] which was one of the last buildings Behrens designed on this site (between 1912 and 1914). Originally, he had a more complex design for this façade of the Assembly Hall, involving a stripped classical portico a little like the Turbine factory. But at the last moment, he decided to open up the north face of the Assembly Hall into three rectangular windows framed by the simplest possible brick moulding, avoiding any specific reference to classical articulation. At the same period he was experimenting with strong juxtapositions of masses in the railway material factory (on the left in **Plate 85**). The way these masses overlap asymmetrically relate back to the more wilful arrangement of some of his earlier buildings influenced by the Viennese architects (Olbrich's Wedding Tower, for instance), while the façade of the Assembly Hall shows us Behrens approaching a completely abstract and sophisticated industrial style, exempt from formalistic influences. The television programme attempts to show how sophisticated Behrens could be in the handling of brick, steel and glass, and how, particularly in the flank of the Assembly Hall, he developed curtain wall systems which were, if anything, more functional and 'serious' than Gropius's. But we should also remember that Behrens was continually haunted by the past—both the recent past of his Darmstadt experience, and the classical past of the German Schinkelesque tradition. We must remember that AEG was a gigantic and powerful commercial empire, and that Rathenau had no delusions about the need to give his buildings the stamp of authority and dignity. It is also important to remember that were it not for the grand monumental effects which Behrens sought—the great pediments and stripped classical articulation systems—we would not be able to find much to interest us in the amazing austerity and simplicity of his details [**Plate 86**]. Seen close to, the undecorated brick walls look completely abstract. It is only when we view the building as a whole that we can read the logical classical language (pilasters, entablatures, pediments, even capitals) out of which the articulation is composed. The main impact created by the High Tension factory (film strip frame 7), with the subtle differences in the colour of the brick between the side wings and the central shed façades, and the spectacular break-back of the three blocks, creates a most powerful architectural sensation—undeniably impressive if overwhelming in scale. This is exactly the kind of value that Lindner and Steinmetz admired (*Documents*, no. 5.3) and that most of the German theorists were searching for.

4   Walter Gropius and Fagus

Compared to that massive effect, Gropius and Meyer's Fagus factory [**Plates 87–93**] makes a much more subtle and delicate impression. For a start the building is much smaller and the tonality of the bricks is much lighter (film strip frame 8). Gropius insisted on a blond yellow brick which escaped the grim industrial quality of the AEG red brick surfaces. The other immediate impression is, of course, that the walls have been dissolved away to become sheets of glass, particularly at the corners. We will look at this building quite closely in the television programme, so there is no need to analyse it in detail here. One point to note, however, is that the transparency of the exterior is carried on into the interior office partitions [**Plate 93**]. These are the offices along the south east side of the administration block, built between 1913–14, and preserved practically untouched since then. Many of the fittings, for example the filing cabinets, looked original.[1] Karl Benscheidt, the founder, knew the United States well, having been there in 1910 collecting funds and ideas, and he may have been influenced by some of the American open plan offices which were already quite common in New York and Chicago. The value of the glass partitions was seen not only as a means of spreading the sunlight even further into the interior, for health and aesthetic reasons, but also to make everyone aware of everyone else in the offices, to encourage hard work and avoid idleness.

It is difficult to realize how intimately the manufacture of shoe lasts was tied in to new concepts of health and improved education. Karl Benscheidt was a sickly child and fanatically keen on using every scientific advance to counteract diseases and bodily distortions. He wrote articles on the subject and made his first shoe lasts by hand while still a student. They were so successful that he set up in business in Hanover, making special shoe lasts for crippled or abnormal feet. Finally, he was offered a job by Carl Behrens, the owner of one of the few major factories in Europe at that time attempting to mass produce wooden shoe lasts. Carl Behrens's plant was alongside the railway tracks at Alfeld-an-der-Leine. On the death of Behrens in 1896, Benscheidt took over the management of this firm in partnership with Wilhelm Bertram, but by 1910, Benscheidt had decided to set up his own company. He applied to the United Shoe Machinery Corporation of America for backing (800,000 marks) and founded the Fagus shoe last factory just across the railway tracks from Behrens and Co. in March 1911. The main point of this is that, like Rathenau at AEG, Benscheidt had direct experience of manufacture with earlier plant and buildings, and had very definite ideas on what improvements were needed. But whereas Rathenau was mainly concerned with extracting the maximum productivity from the available sites, which were cramped anyway due to their big city

[1] We visited *the* factory in 1973.

Figure 50   Edouard Werner, original scheme for Fagus factory approved, April, 1911.

(a) *Plan*

(b) *Elevation, north-east façade*

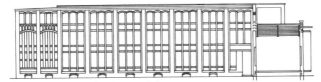

location, Benscheidt from the start insisted that his workers should enjoy every advantage that modern American industrial planning could offer: well ventilated machine shops, a strictly linear throughput in plan to minimize unnecessary transportation, and comfortable and well lit offices and studios for his clerks and draughtsmen. The factory was seen from the start as an agent for social change and new standards of hygiene, visibly preaching a gospel of reformed living. The architect commissioned to give physical form to this brief was Eduard Werner, who had a reputation as an industrial architect in the Hanover area. His plans and elevations [**Fig. 50**] were approved by Benscheidt and passed by the building authorities in April 1911. Work was begun on the foundations in May. So where was Gropius?

With Prussian determination, Gropius had been engaged throughout the last months of 1910 in a campaign of letter writing to all the conceivable potential clients he could think of, using as part of his publicity the fame of the AEG buildings, on which he had worked as an assistant in Peter Behrens's office. The letter he wrote to Karl Benscheidt in December 1911, contained references to the fact that he had had the opportunity, under Behrens, of working out 'an artistically and practically thought through project', and gave as a reference his brother-in-law, Herr Burchard, in Alfeld. It is probably just as well that Gropius had these two cards up his sleeve, since Werner had already been commissioned, as Benscheidt explained in a letter to Gropius of 12 January 1911. Benscheidt made it quite clear that he had known Werner for several years and that his plan and general arrangement for the factory could not be improved upon. But he continued:

I have a different opinion, however, of the external form of the building. Here perhaps the man in question has not carried out my wishes completely, and if you are indeed ready to collaborate on this project, I would be happy to avail myself of your services.

(Weber, *op. cit.*, recommended reading, p. 3)

Figure 51   Walter Gropius, revised plan for first building phase of Fagus factory, approved September 1911.

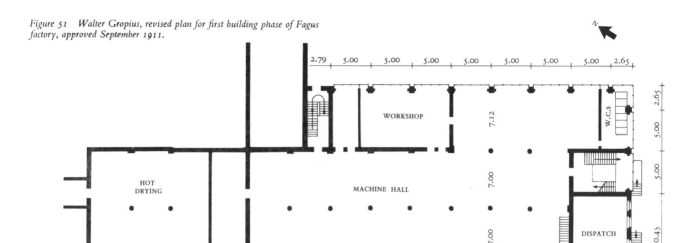

(b) Elevation drawing, north-east façade

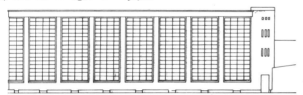

After a visit to Alfeld and further consultation, Benscheidt sent Gropius a stack of Werner's finished plans and drawings on 20 March, with an accompanying note which included these words: 'I am asking you now to examine these plans, to see what you could make of the façade'. It was in response to this that Gropius worked out his elevation drawing of the façade [**Fig. 51b**], with a section to show how it worked. On 24 April, Gropius signed an agreement in Alfeld, in which he insisted on his control over every aspect of the exterior appearance of the building, despite the fact that the Werner elevations were four days from receiving official authorization. Gropius's plans and elevations were not approved until September, although building work had continued during the summer according to the changed scheme. The first part of the factory, towards the north east, was completed in 1912, and in 1913 Benscheidt was ready to double up the area of the factory, which was completed by 1914. Look at **Figures 50a** and **b** and **51a** and **b** which compare the Werner and Gropius plans and façade elevations (note also **Figs. 52 and 53**).

1 What major changes did Gropius introduce in the 1911–12 part of the building?

2 Are there any significant changes in plan?

● 1 The most striking change is in the façade, as requested by Benscheidt. Werner's façade elevation was predominantly of brick, or that is the impression it gives, while Gropius's façade seems to have beeen dissolved

Figure 52   Walter Gropius, plan of the south-east wing of the administration block, the extension to the 1911–12 section (plan officially approved 20 February, 1914), top floor.

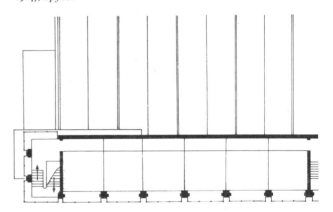

Figure 53   Walter Gropius, part of elevation drawing for Fagus factory, south-east façade of the first section built, (drawing officially approved September 1911).

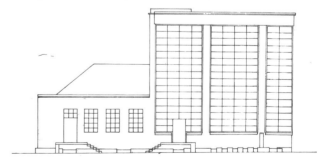

altogether. It is difficult to make head or tail of it at a first glance. It is interesting, though, to see how similar the plans are, even down to the placing of the brick piers along the north east side. Gropius's most spectacular change in the layout of the piers was at the corner, where, instead of doubling the rhythm of the windows as Werner had done, and lengthening the stride of the last bay (from 5·0 metres to a big one of 7·52 metres), Gropius simply carried on his 5 metre bay for one more interval, leaving himself with half (2·65 metres), which he decided to treat as if it was a whole one bent round the corner. The main impact of the Gropius façade is further made possible by extending the line of the windows 30 odd centimetres outside the line of the brick piers, instead of the normal arrangement of setting them inside the line of the external wall. This may not look very important on the plan, or even in the elevation drawing, but it makes all the difference to the appearance, because the glass windows unite together visually to form a sheet of uninterrupted glass, whenever the angle of sight is at all oblique to the wall. This phenomenon is shown in the programme.

2 The changes in the overall plan were minimal. Notice that Gropius's plan was smaller in area by one bay towards the south west. This was simply for reasons of economy. It had always been planned to double up the factory as soon as funds permitted, and this extension in fact took place during 1913–14, when the south east face of the administrative block was completed [**Fig. 52**] and all the other parts of the factory extended along this front. Otherwise, the main change in the plan is that Gropius was unwilling to follow Werner's practice of having a different bay width for the south east façade (3·50 metres) than that on the north east façade (5 metres). Werner did this mainly because it respected the 5 by 7 metre module of the manufacturing shed. But Gropius was forced to continue his 5 metre module because of the glass corner, since this simply extended it round the corner from one façade to the other. It did not make much odds when only two and a half bays of the south east glass wall were completed [**Fig. 53**], but there were some more odd results when the whole façade was finished between 1913 and 1914 [**Fig. 52**], mainly because the structural grid was broken. ●

Notice how, in the later building extension [**Fig. 52**], the staircase was really tacked on to the end of the building for completely aesthetic reasons. The staircases in the first building part [**Fig. 51a**], were much more modest, supported between brick walls, but at the south corner of the building, facing the entrance to the factory, Gropius wanted to use his new trick of the glazed corner and combine it with a dramatically exposed staircase to show off the self-supporting glass wall. The staircase is of steel, cantilevered and braced so that it does not even touch the glass wall.

Two final points about the Fagus factory: Gropius made many changes to Werner's elevation drawings in the surface treatment of the other buildings in the factory, using rendered and brick surfaces with great economy. In this he was fortunate in having the help of his partner,

Adolf Meyer, who was an experienced industrial architect, and to whom one should attribute most of the detailing of the building. The glass windows of the administrative building had to be specially made, with hand made welded and bolted frames, and glass which had to be specially ordered because the size of the panes was so large. The quality of workmanship throughout the factory is superb and has survived very well. The factory still runs under the management of Benscheidt's son, and the processes and even some of the machinery, have remained substantially the same, despite the introduction of a line in cheaper plastic lasts as well as the wooden ones. The Fagus factory must be seen as an extremely unified conception, in terms of the overall aims of the production, the methods and materials used and the built environment created to house them. Whether or not one should see a major divide between Behrens's factories and Gropius's, it is quite clear that aesthetically, Gropius discovered an imagery here which has been a central one for modern architecture ever since. It is worth looking carefully at his description of the proper relationship between architect and client in industry (*Form and Function*, no. 26) from just this period, to see how closely it described what happened at the Fagus factory.

5 German design before the Werkbund

In Part Three we looked at how the values of craftsmanship and simplicity were being emphasized in Austria and Darmstadt. In Germany, there were workshops operating in a similar vein. Two of the most important ones were at Munich and Dresden. (Read pages 32–4 in *Pevsner*.) The artists and designers in Austria and Darmstadt had been concerned with establishing a quality and style in design that was orientated towards the monied and élite classes. Nevertheless, this did not on the whole affect the general public, or the economic position of Germany in the way that the expansion in some industrial concerns (like the steel industry) had done. These two elements, quality and economy, were combined by Karl Schmidt, who was the pioneer in Germany of the development that enabled the practical requirements of everyday life to be produced with an awareness of visual aesthetics, quality and economy.

6 Dresden, 1905

Karl Schmidt had started his Dresden *Werkstätte für Handwerkskunst* (Workshops for Handcrafts) in 1898 on the same lines as the Munich *Jugendstil* designers had begun their workshop a little earlier. But his was more a purely commercial concern than the English Arts and Crafts workshops, and right from the beginning Schmidt was thinking, more than the other reformers, in terms of making good products of the new style available to a greater number of people. He worked in close conjunction with the editors of the reformist periodical, *Der Kunstwart*, and his ideas were akin to the neo-vernacular advocates, like Schultze-Naumburg and Lichtwark. During 1906-7, most of the reformist German workshops amalgamated in the *Deutsche Werkstätten* under Schmidt's directorship and established themselves in Hellerau Garden City, near Dresden.

In Schmidt's workshops at Dresden, the machine was used as a tool. It did not dominate the design, nor were the objects produced merely trying to ape hand made objects. In other words, the methods of making an object were adapted towards the machine. Encouraged by Karl Schmidt, Richard Riemerschmid developed a great variety of furniture that was made by machine, using mostly the saw and milling machines. The saw was used for cutting the basic shapes, while the milling machine was used for bevelling and creating plastic forms. Riemerschmid accepted the fact, that at that time machines were not sufficiently accurate to be able to cut wood to fit exactly into a tongue and groove joint, so all the joints were overlapped and screwed, rather than being let in. This also meant that the furniture could be transported to its destination in pieces and then screwed together by an unskilled worker, or a buyer, on arrival. This sort of furniture was made in three different price ranges, the cheapest costing 450 marks, made out of pine wood, and the most expensive 24,000 marks. A series of 'completion' furniture was also designed, in which a piece of furniture, such as a bookcase, could be added to or expanded at a later date. Schmidt and Riemerschmid realized that skilled labour was becoming more and more expensive, so that the new, simply designed and well made furniture like that produced at Vienna was going to be very expensive when hand made. Throughout the nineteenth century, hand made objects were only available to the few, and this trend would increase as time passed. They also felt that the aristocratic 'stamp' of modern decorative design was in contradiction to the aims of making it simple in form. Design had not adjusted to the new social conditions. They were also aware that the actual name 'machine furniture' was going to put some people off, because previously the machine had had nothing to do with art, at least for the majority of the public. Schmidt and Riemerschmid overcame the major problems of ornate designs unsuitable for machinery by emphasizing the 'noble simplicity' (a term Winckelmann had used in the eighteenth century about classical art) of their designs and constructing them in a way that did not emphasize certain inaccuracies in machine production. A designer would personally supervise a piece of design from beginning to end—including, for example, the design of the fabric covering of a chair.

Another element which had discouraged the use of machinery, was the possibility of having many designed objects which were all identical and might become boring —something that was certainly not experienced in Vienna, where the monogram of the artist was applied to each individually designed piece. The element of anonymous design had to be accepted, if machine made objects were to succeed. There was an increasing awareness of anonymous design: already, by the end of the nineteenth century, America was manufacturing mass-produced work designed by people specially trained as designers. There was also in Germany a general trend towards admiring the anonymous forms of both the peasant designer and the actual forms of machinery, from turbines to cars.

Nevertheless, this was a new concept for the public of Dresden to assimilate in 1904, and Schmidt was worried about people feeling that the designs were too monotonous. His answer was to run a particular style for one year only and then change it. **What are the implications of this idea?**

● The whole concept of styling in relation to economy and mass production evolves around this idea, which reached a peak in the 1930s in American car styling and is very much a part of our economy today. It is easy to see which is an outdated design, and so pressure is put on society always to be up to date and fashionable, and to buy new things when, as far as function or comfort are concerned, the older things are perfectly adequate. It emphasizes visually the income bracket of the people and ideas like 'eat below your means and dress above them.' It shows that industry was never going to act as a force for standardization and concentration on a few, universal good forms, as some theorists had hoped. ●

7 Germany and Austria

In Germany and Austria at the end of the nineteenth century, there was a strong art emphasis in design education. You have already looked at the results of some of these attitudes in the Wiener Werkstätte. This had just been reinforced by a movement towards more creative expression by schoolchildren—things like music, gym and art became as important as the more academic subjects. Part of this was due to the popularity of the Froebel–Montessori method of free expression, letting the child develop his own creative abilities without having adult criteria imposed on him. This attitude was reinforced by the English Arts and Crafts principle of doing rather than learning, and is closely paralleled by the development of the psychology of empathy. Many of the future members of the Deutscher Werkbund were particularly involved in this attitude towards education and it soon spread to the art schools, especially at Hamburg, under Alfred Lichtwark. At the same time craft classes were being introduced in art schools, as they had been in England. In some cases, for example in Munich, this had happened in the 1880s when pottery, metal and textile schools were introduced. So by introducing the crafts to the German art schools where artists attempted to teach craftsmen already employed in industry, they were imposing a style on objects which had been relatively traditional before.

Many painters and architects were put at the head of the newly organized applied arts schools at the beginning of the twentieth century, one of whom was Behrens, appointed head of the Düsseldorf school. His attitude towards the training of designers was typical of the time; he said: 'Impressions experienced should in every case be made the point of departure for stylized form'. This attitude was very much in keeping with the Froebel–Montessori method, but this deliberate application of art to craft, was later to bedevil attempts to design for industry in Germany. This attitude can be seen partly as a result of artists turning to craft and partly due to the use of craft as a part of art education, where simple learning by making is exploited to get round problems of teaching technique and self-expression.

By 1906, many workshops were becoming large and successful, and economic factors were coming more to the fore. The emphasis on art and the form of the objects, was still very important, but people were becoming more aware that they were not facing up to the problems of their times. By 1905, cars were to be seen reasonably frequently on the roads and had been mass-produced in America since 1896. The German economy needed the production of more cheap, good articles and the move towards this approach was made by Hermann Muthesius, an architect and critic who had been in England between 1896–1903. Already in 1903, Schmidt had had discussions with him over the running of the Dresden workshop and before this, in 1901, Muthesius had said:

Let the human mind think of shapes the machine can produce. Such shapes, once they are logically developed in accordance with what machines can do, we may certainly call artistic. They will satisfy because they will no longer be imitation of handicraft, but typical machine made shapes.

In this statement, the emphasis is on shapes, in other words, the aesthetics. The biggest resistance to machine production came from people who had been indoctrinated into considering only the craftsmanship in design. To them it was the art or design of the object that was important in the sense that it betrayed the soul of the creator. Perhaps this helps to explain why, when mass-produced furniture was first made at Dresden, there was an emphasis put on the spirit of the machine. This 'spirit' was to substitute for the human soul, thereby romanticizing and humanizing the machine to render it more acceptable. Basically, the change

in criteria from hand made to machine made objects was one which put much more emphasis on the visual form. It was no longer possible to say, like William Morris, that something was good because it was well made, and the craftsmanship sound. When the machine was involved these criteria were nullified. This perhaps helps to explain the concern for the formal properties and visually based criteria that were so important to Muthesius, and was to lead to the search for absolute laws of good proportion, and the properties of colour, line and texture.

Look back at the furniture designs produced by the Werkstätte. Do they look as if they could have been made by machinery? There are none of the complex, curvilinear shapes and decoration that are found in, say, Gaudí's or Guimard's furniture (which sometimes had to be made from clay models, since the design was too complex for working drawings to be made). Because of the stress on simplicity and good materials in the Arts and Crafts Movement, designers felt that they already had forms that could be machine made, and it is only in their theories and writings that the anti-machine element comes over. They did not realize that to design for machine production is a completely different process from handwork, and that forms which are simple and satisfactory in handwork are not necessarily so in machine production. Nevertheless, a change could be made towards accepting the machine, if there was sufficient theoretical proof of its value. This took the form of equating geometrical order with a machine aesthetic. You have seen earlier in these units how important clean geometric forms were becoming for designers, even before machine made objects were considered.

8 Hermann Muthesius (1861–1927)

Hermann Muthesius had studied English design and architecture intensively; the Kaiser, who was one of Queen Victoria's grandsons, took a personal interest in his stay in England (1896–1903). On his return to Germany, three large, illustrated volumes entitled *Das englische Haus* (The English house) were published by Ernst Wasmuth in 1904–5 (see *Form and Function*, no. 17). In these volumes there is not only a discussion of buildings, but sections on plumbing, furniture and even details of window fittings and the construction of fire grates and flues.

While Muthesius was in England, he observed the rejection of Mackintosh's work and the difficulties experienced by Ashbee's Guild of Handicraft. It is also important that Muthesius designed some buildings and furniture himself. He had originally studied at the Berlin Technical College in the 1880s, where the architectural training was very much more technical than it was in England and Vienna at that time. On his return to Germany in 1904, he was made Inspector of the Prussian Ministry of

Trade and Industry and thus came face to face with the Werkstätte situation.

9 Behrens's design for the AEG

The awareness of the need of both art for industry and especially industry for art had been flirted with in Austria and Germany up to 1907. In that year, Behrens, who had left Darmstadt to become head of the Düsseldorf School of Art, was asked by Paul Jordan, the technical director of AEG to do for the factory what had been done already by the Werkstätte for domestic interior design; in other words, to bring a unity of good design to their products— a corporate identity.

Part of the reason for this industrial patronage of the arts was economic. German industry needed an economic boost. AEG realized that electricity was very much a source of power with a future in the twentieth century, and that therefore they needed to bring the whole of their visual image in line with the now accepted simplicity of craftsmanship. The man behind this move was Emil Rathenau, director of AEG. He held a powerful position in German economics and politics and believed that the capitalist ought to be the prime patron of art and design, not by decorating his own house, or by donating a fresco to the local library, but by improving the aesthetic aspects of his product. Architects had often been employed by industrialists to design ornaments for their buildings or products (in Berlin this had been customary since the time of Schinkel). AEG had employed the well established Berlin architect Franz Schwechten (1841–1924) and the Art Nouveau designer, Otto Eckmann, but Behrens was the first architect to be employed with the object of creating a consistent visual image for AEG, from the design

of the actual products to the design of the 'logo'. Schwechten had made an effort in this direction but his ideas were bounded by the confines of the neo-Gothic style. His logo for AEG [**Fig. 54**] seems light years away from that of Behrens [**Fig. 55**]. In talking about his design work for AEG, Behrens was keen to point out that they were really trying to come to terms with the design of everyday objects. They were not involved in *Kunstgewerbe*, but in down-to-earth industrial design. He saw that the new design for AEG arc lamps (illustrated in *Pevsner*, Fig. 136) was simple, and the form of the object respected the form necessary for efficient functioning. Nevertheless, electric and gas lamps had been produced for the past twenty years by anonymous designers for several firms, including AEG, which look fairly similar to Behrens's. The difference in these AEG designs is that they were being deliberately promoted as examples of good 'artistic design'. The public were told that these were in 'good taste'. By attempting to redesign the rest of the AEG products, such as cookers, kettles, etc. [**Fig. 56**], in a similarly artistic and sophisticated way, AEG thought they were improving the economy of the country by establishing a national sense of good taste. Notice, however, that these electric kettles are not all of the simple, smooth kind like the one illustrated in *Pevsner*, Fig. 135. The one in **Fig. 56**, has an imitation hammered surface and mouldings composed of little balls. The Arts and Crafts ideals were far from dead but many of the AEG products commit the cardinal sin of imitating hand craftsmanship, using mechanical means of

Figure 55 Peter Behrens, A.E.G. Logo, 1908.

Figure 54 Franz Schwechten, A.E.G. Logo, 1903.

production. In talking about a simplification in design for mass-produced, everyday objects, Behrens was applying some of the ideas that had already been established in the

Figure 56   Peter Behrens, electric teapot, c. 1910.

Figure 57   Peter Behrens, electric fans designed for A.E.G., 1913.

Arts and Crafts in Austria and Germany. Not all the AEG designs were to be as straightforward as the electric fans [**Fig. 57**]; some designs were intended for a more expensive price range, being made out of pinchbeck (zinc and copper alloy), like the covers for heating elements [**Fig. 58**] designed in 1909. These are ornamented, but with geometric forms. The metal has a hand beaten quality about it: in fact, these look rather like Arts and Crafts objects. Behrens pointed out that a slightly more expensive material justified the use of ornament—but only 'impersonal', geometric ornament. It should be remembered that electricity itself was rare and expensive at this time. AEG publicity material from this period shows illustrations of domestic servants using the pieces of domestic electric equipment. The kind of family who could not afford servants could not afford electric gadgets in the house either.

Figure 58   Peter Behrens, electric stoves for A.E.G. 1909.

In trying to give a very definite house-style to AEG, Behrens was also putting over a particular style and attitude that would be seen by a large number of people (AEG organized further education courses about industrial design). He designed the shop fronts for the AEG shops in Berlin [**Fig. 59**] in a severe, noble style, where the typography is clean and simple, both in the form of the individual letters and in the placing of these letters on the façade. The large, clear glass front of the shop is geometrically balanced by the surrounding rectangular elements and the actual display in the shop window is very

Figure 59   Peter Behrens, A.E.G. sales room in Potsdamerstrasse, Berlin, 1900.

Figure 61   Peter Behrens, A.E.G. banner, designed 1912.

Figure 60   Peter Behrens, cover of an A.E.G. brochure in 3 colours, 1908.

arbiters of taste, and of their role in building up Germany's economy. The clean AEG logo is clearly displayed on the end façade of the Turbine factory. Look at the development of the AEG logos from the original one produced by Schwechten in 1903 [**Fig. 54**] through the Behrens design on the brochure of 1908 [**Fig. 60**], to his logo of the same year [**Fig. 55**] and finally to the banner of 1912 [**Fig. 61**]. **What developments do you notice?**

● It is difficult to read the actual letters of Schwechten's logo. Behrens's brochure design, although cleaner and more geometric in the general layout is still ornamented, like the covers for the heating elements. It retains an Arts and Crafts interest in calligraphy and the hand of the artist in the central AEG logo. The other logo by Behrens, done in the same year, has a monumental directness that shows a confidence and acceptance of simple forms. The letters themselves are beginning to become the main part of the design. The banner of 1912 contains no ornamentation at all. The design consists of the play of the spacing of the letters, and their simple, heavy forms. The exaggerated spacing of the letters in the upper and lower lines betrays the artistic conception of the design, and could be compared with the stylish simplicity of Hoffmann's chairs. The letters also have a more rounded contour than at first meets the eye. As in his typefaces, Behrens was always looking for some redeeming warmth in the generally severe tone he wanted to set. ●

consciously symmetrically arranged. Such design would be seen by many and would begin to take on the role of 'trendsetter'. If a large important firm were using clean, simple forms, this idea must be acceptable. In the same way that the Deutscher Werkbund tried to educate the public, Behrens and AEG were likewise conscious of becoming

A firm which patronized many of the most interesting German designers of the time was Anker Linoleum Co. (film strip frames 11 and 12). Behrens's linoleum pattern, composed entirely of squares and circles, but brilliantly decorative in its effect, shows a more complete expression of the disciplines of industrial design than anything produced by AEG.

10 The Deutscher Werkbund

Read *Banham*, Chapter 5 and *Form and Function*, nos. 19, 20, 23, 24 and 25. One of the most powerful ways the Werkbund could immediately try to affect design was through a thorough rethinking and reorganization of design education. They had to try to persuade industry that it was an economically viable proposition to be involved in what the Werkbund considered good design. This was no easy task, for it must still have seemed unnecessarily 'arty' to many industries. Secondly, the Werkbund had to educate the public and retailers. If the public did not demand or appreciate this good design, there would be no market for it in Germany. This, therefore, affected the retailers, who were only interested in the saleability of their wares. An extensive programme of evening lectures, not on style or art history, but on the nature of different materials, the pros and cons of using hand labour or machinery, technical conditions and requirements, were arranged in many towns with supporting exhibitions.

Membership of the Deutscher Werkbund was kept select, applicants being first vetted by one local person and one professional expert. It soon came to be regarded as a mark of quality to have 'DWB' on one's notepaper. By 1909 there were 731 members: 360 artists, 267 manufacturers and traders and 95 experts. Nevertheless, there were some cases of non-cooperation from industry and trade schools and this called for a certain amount of bribery by the Werkbund. In Württemberg, state premiums were granted to master craftsmen who gave their apprentices a good training and allowed them time to learn from the DWB. Many of the trade schools were not cooperative for they could not see that it was their individual job to arrest the decline of industry; and few of them had sufficiently qualified teachers. It was to their nationalistic pride that the appeal went out. More industries were subsidized by the DWB, and a museum of industrial design was founded at Hagen. By 1909, the DWB was beginning to look more towards objects for a lower class of people.

In 1909, Riemerschmid and Bertsch developed the *Typenmöbel* furniture at Munich [**Plates 94** and **95**]. The basis of this furniture was well worked out and tested types of construction whereby one form of, say, an arm, could be replaced by another form, or the same form in a different type of wood. This meant that there could be a large number of different permutations and combinations, and 800 different kinds of chairs could be made in large quantities and relatively cheaply, using machine labour. But, as Riemerschmid was keen to point out, the whole process ensured that the furniture had an 'individuality and character of its own, without betraying the use of machinery in its production'. The main reforms were to

do with the organization of labour and the use of more machine-turned parts, rather than the overall form. If you look at the *Typenmöbel* chairs by K. Bertsch [**Plate 95**] they look very similar to the chairs produced at Darmstadt by Behrens in 1901, and certainly from just looking at them you would not guess which one had been machine made.

To the DWB designers who were designing for mass production, Muthesius's ideas[1] were acceptable and formed the criteria of this new discipline. But there is a completely different discipline involved in designing for mass production, compared with hand production. If you make one chair by hand and nobody wants to buy it you are left with just one chair, but if you make 200 chairs by mass production and nobody likes them it is a very different financial loss. This fact was only just realized in Germany in 1914, when it was pointed out that artists are always striving for tomorrow's new idea, which is a principle too risky for mass production. Therefore the designer of mass-produced goods must work within a very different framework from the artist. Before the war, most artists saw themselves as artists rather than industrial designers.

Some Deutscher Werkbund designers

Bruno Paul, a designer and architect associated with the Munich workshops was a very versatile designer, turning his hand to most things. The carpet design [**Fig. 62**] was made for mass production by a Berlin firm. The repetitive circular motif set within a geometric grid is a design that could well have been derived from a study of flower forms, but it is very different from the realistic flower patterns of Morris.

We looked at Henry van de Velde's early career in Units 3–4. The window display of his Tropon posters, 1913 [**Fig. 63**, see also Units 3–4, Fig. 51] shows him still using the Art Nouveau graphic style of his earlier posters,

Figure 62 Bruno Paul, Hand-made smyrna carpet.

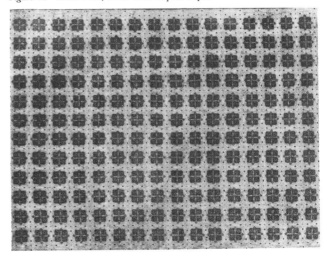

---

[1] E.g. *Form and Function*, nos. 19, 24 and 25. Read what Banham has to say about these in Chapter 5 (set book).

but there is a different quality in this illustration, since it is symmetrically and geometrically organized, while the central poster has a Neoclassical clarity that shows how far he has moved away from Art Nouveau ideas. Many of the DWB designers were involved in window display and the design of shop fronts. Van de Velde's later designs for cutlery [**Plate 96**] by 1912 reveal the fact that he had now accepted, to a certain extent, simple, clean forms. His design for a sideboard in 1906 [**Plate 97**] has a monolithic

Figure 63   Henry Van de Velde, display for Tropon, 1913.

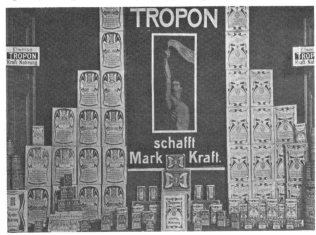

(b) Josef Hoffmann, Linoleum design, Ankermarke

(c) Henry Van de Velde, Linoleum design, Ankermarke

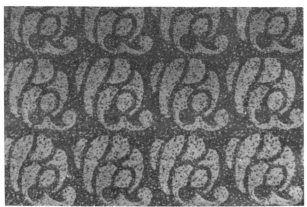

symmetry and clarity, and a concern for clean geometric forms and limpid surfaces. The leading on the glass panels and the cut glass itself could be compared to some of Behrens's Oldenburg exhibition designs, with their strong emphasis on geometry. But his wall lights remind us how different his formal imagination normally was to that of Behrens [**Plate 98**]. The period that Walter Gropius (1883–1969), spent in Behrens's office reveals itself in the study he designed in 1912 [**Plate 99**]. It shows a love of clean, hard forms, but still retains a feeling for hand craftsmanship in the super-polished treatment of the wood. Some other designs by DWB members:

Shelter by R. Grimm [**Plate 100**]. This is an outstanding design which would have been easy to construct and shows remarkable similarities to the style of Hoffmann's Palais Stoclet in Brussels. This sort of bus shelter only appeared in England in the 1930s when it was thought to be a very revolutionary design by London Transport.

Interior of a tram by A. Grenander [**Plate 101**]. Apart from the unity of this design there is an interesting feature in the use of continuous chromed metal for the arm rests, which show a similarity to some of the elements in bentwood furniture. Many of the most 'serious' advances in industrial design were associated with public transport.

Bedroom by Paul Schultze-Naumburg [**Plate 102**]. In this interior, the Neoclassical and *Biedermeier* elements are very much evident, especially in the couch, dressing table and heavily draped long windows.

Wallpapers designed by E. Seyfried for mass production [**Fig. 64**]. These look as if they could have been designed much earlier and printed by woodcuts. At this time woodcut illustrations were being revived, an idea which closely parallels the revival of the vernacular and the new interest in calligraphy, and which emphasizes the fact that craftsmanship was still a strong element in the DWB.

To end our round-up of designs by members of the Werkbund, we have illustrated an electric lamp by Riemerschmid from 1906, the year before the Werkbund was founded [**Plate 103**].

The Deutscher Werkbund and graphic design

The main influence on graphic art came from England, particularly in the sphere of typography and calligraphy. Edward Johnston and his pupils at the Central School of Art in London had tried to revive the skills of hand lettering, incorporating the best qualities of hand formed letters into typefaces, but striving for a clear, elegant face. In Germany, the work of Johnston and the private presses in England encouraged patrons like Count Harry Kessler to improve the typefaces of their own presses on similar lines. Muthesius arranged for Johnston to give lectures in Dresden, and you can see the kind of effects he admired

Figure 64   E. Seyfried, wallpaper, 1914.

Figure 66   Rudolf Koch, monogram, 1913.

Figure 67   F. P. Glass, poster for 'Die Sechs', Munich, 1914.

from a photograph of the blackboard [**Fig. 65**], at the end of one of Johnston's lectures. Rudolf Koch was also a great admirer of Johnston but he developed a very personal and individualistic approach to typography [**Fig. 66**], using the letters to express the character and soul of the creator. Despite some efforts to design new faces suitable for general usage, most designers were preoccupied with the formal problems of good proportion, expressiveness and character in typography.

We find similar characteristics in the work of graphic artists associated with the Deutscher Werkbund. 'The Six' were a group of designers in Munich who specialized in high quality printing and the use of primary colours and bold forms [**Figs. 67–69** and film strip frames 9 and 10].

Figure 65   Edward Johnston, blackboard after lecture at Dresden, 1912.

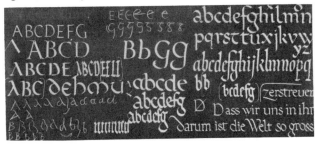

Figure 68   F. Heubner, poster for 'Die Sechs', Munich, 1914.

Figure 69   M. Schwarzer, poster for 'Die Sechs', Munich.

They were not held together by any stylistic uniformity, but worked in collaboration with United Printers whom they could trust to print their work well. They charged 250 marks for a commission, and for this, each designer would produce a rough, the client would choose the one he preferred, and this would then be printed up by United Printers and the fee divided equally between the six designers. The client thus had the choice of six fairly varied and individual works. The posters illustrated here were intended to advertise The Six and they give a good idea of the imagery of the period. Bold, clear colours, a strong impact and the use of stylized floral motifs rather like some peasant decorative idioms. They are all using the poster as a method of communication, rather than as a picture with some lettering on it and they show that the lessons of Art Nouveau posters had not been lost.

11   The Cologne Exhibition, 1914

In 1914, the DWB finally appeared on show in a large exhibition in Cologne. Its membership was over a thousand, and in one year it had organized fifty travelling exhibitions, six of which had been sent to America. The Werkbund at Cologne showed a very varied selection of work. There

was a complete housing estate with youth centre; a shopping street; pavilions for transport, and for the care of the ill and incurable; a model factory designed by Gropius that contained seventy working machine exhibits; and a main hall of 242 units. It was thought at the time that much of the architecture was disappointing, and that only three buildings were of outstanding interest: Gropius's factory, Bruno Taut's Glass Pavilion, and Van de Velde's theatre. Before examining these three buildings, look at some of the other pavilions [**Plates 104–106**]. **What do you notice in particular about the style of these buildings?**

● Each one has a strong monumental form which in some way adheres to a classical tradition. Compare Hoffmann's Austrian pavilion with Behrens's pavilion. Hoffmann is using a clean, well articulated form, similar to his Primavesi house [**Plates 56–58**] with bulky, fluted pilasters that have no capitals. The lettering on the building is in a formalistic Viennese typeface, mounted on stepped-back plinths under the pediments. The pavilion is more or less the architectural equivalent of his chairs and is more to do with a very self-conscious stylistic use of geometric forms than with the details of the classical vocabulary, but

Figure 70   B. Taut, Glass Pavilion, Cologne Exhibition, 1914, Plan.

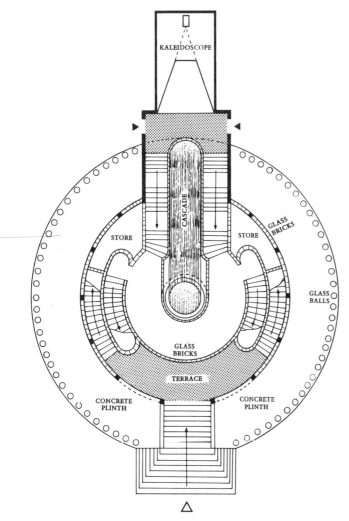

we can still identify specific classical features, such as pediments, pilasters and so forth. The grandiose bombast of Fascist Neoclassical architecture does not seem far away. Peter Behrens's pavilion [**Plate 105**], too, is decidedly classical in its general arrangement, with the central section of the façade arranged in the forms of a Roman triumphal arch. The rather classical sculpture increases the illusion. The sides are more abstract, with long vertical windows, lighting the staircase, but we still feel that the treatment is based firmly on a Schinkelesque Neoclassicism. Muthesius's pavilion [**Plate 104**], is the least overtly Neoclassical, but retains the sort of classical logic in its dome, portico and pilasters. All three buildings can be thus described in classical terms and have the look of serious, imposing nationalist architecture of the kind normally used for embassies (like the Petrograd Embassy) or art galleries. ●

The three buildings by Gropius, Van de Velde and Taut are clearly different [**Plates 107–114** and **Fig. 70**]. Gropius's

Model Factory is arguably one of the key turning points in the development of modern architecture, following on from the Fagus factory in an apparently logical progression. This, at least, is Pevsner's view (pp. 215–17), as you know. Banham (pp. 85–7) endeavoured to modify this view considerably. And in Units 9–10 we will have to come back to this building and put it into the context of post-war developments. Similarly, we will have to return to Taut's Glass Pavilion and Van de Velde's theatre in the context of Expressionism, also in Units 9–10. But it would be useful for you to make detailed notes now on the following questions before the link with the other contemporary pre-war developments is broken.

1   Do these three buildings have anything in common, particularly by comparison with the other pavilions?

2   Do they seem more or less characteristic of developments generally in this period than the other three pavilions we looked at earlier?

3   Which of them do you suppose would be most influential on the architecture of the immediate post-war period?

4   What do you think of this reaction by the young Eric Mendelsohn (who will play a big part in Units 9–10 and 11–12):

Peter Behrens fails completely. This step backwards, after his Turbine factory, almost convinces one of the chance nature of that creation, which perhaps owed its birth to the constructional genius of one of his engineers. Only Van de Velde, with his theatre, is really searching for form. Concrete used in the *Jugendstil* way, but strong in conception and expression. Gropius, with his factory, is already in search of something new. Hoffmann, Vienna, in the Austrian Pavilion . . . remains, despite the rhythmical verve, under the spell of the Greek temple, and creates columns where he should be finding structural elements that are appropriate to the new perceptions of statics.

(Letter of 11 September 1914 from Eric Mendelsohn, *Letters of an Architect*, Oscar Beyer (ed.), Abelard Schuman, 1967)

● We will look at Taut's Glass Pavilion and Van de Velde's theatre in detail in Units 9–10, since they are key works concerned with ideas that relate to Expressionism. Here, it is important to remember that Taut's seminal Expressionist building occurred in the Cologne exhibition, under the auspices of the Deutscher Werkbund. The use of emotive, expressive elements like light, glass, colour and water, combined in one building with the monumental and enclosed quality of the exterior, shows two of the architectural polarities of the exhibition. But do make a conscientious effort to write down your thoughts on these questions and the whole pre-war situation as expressed at Cologne. Units 7–8, on American architecture will throw some new light on the problem of Gropius's Model Factory, but they will also necessarily come between these units and the continuation of the story in Units 9–10. One thing which should be clear is that, on the evidence of the Cologne exhibition, there was a clear polarization in Europe between a sober, classicist camp (Muthesius, Behrens, Hoffmann) and a more imaginative, individualistic group, characterized by Gropius, Taut and Van de Velde.   •

Some of the design exhibits at Cologne

Let us see whether the same polarization occurs in interior design. Look at the interior room setting by Hoffmann [**Plate 115**], with its regency stripes and strangely mannered chairs, looking almost like a setting for a late Beardsley illustration. The lightness and grace of the Wiener Werkstätte designs seems to be becoming rather fussy and precious. Muthesius's pavilion for the American Hamburg shipping line [**Plate 116**] features glass panels of transparent pictures set within classical temple shapes. But the general mood is of cool, hard, graphic formalism, with each window bay marked out by dark lines against the lighter walls.

The door handles [**Plate 117**] by Behrens, Paul and Lonholdt all have a confident, chunky appearance about them and some form of decoration, often in parallel lines that emphasize the geometry of squares, circles and rectangles. One gets the feeling that all these designs are conceived with *Biedermeier* prototypes in mind. The room interior [**Plate 118**] by Van de Velde, however, with its Art Nouveau chairs and carpet, presents us with a mixture of styles. The large symmetrical bookcase, with its rounded corners, is beginning to look every bit like a 1930s radio cabinet and the walls are treated with a modest patterned paper.

The study by Bruno Paul [**Plate 119**] with the elegant Neoclassical furniture and large net draped windows, has a heavy monumentality in the dark woods and panels that can be compared with Gropius's veneered sideboard [**Plate 120**]. This seems so different from the transparent clarity of his factory at the same exhibition. Remember this sideboard when you look at Gropius's early work at the Bauhaus. There is a slightly jumpy, finicky quality in the wallpapers in both these rooms.

12   The Muthesius–Van de Velde debate

It is not surprising to find that there was a lot of criticism of the exhibition, especially of the furniture. Muthesius said 'foreigners quite rightly feel that much in our modern decorative art is too heavy, bumptious, massive and aggressive'. He felt that the time had come once more to clarify the aims of the DWB, and in 1914 he put forward ten propositions (*Documents*, no. 1.1). Several of the DWB members objected to the tone of these propositions, which they thought emphasized standardization and depersonalizing of design. On the night after Muthesius had announced his propositions, Van de Velde, helped by Taut, Obrist and Endell, sat up and composed a set of counter-propositions in favour of artistic freedom (*Documents*, no. 1.2). Muthesius's speech (*Documents*, no. 1.3) adopted a less aggressive tone, though it may be that he genuinely did not intend to make his propositions as dogmatic as they seemed to most Werkbund members. In the debate which followed (*Documents*, no. 1.4) the issues are further brought down to earth. Eventually votes were taken among the DWB members and Muthesius's memorandum was withdrawn, since the large majority of designers were on Van de Velde's side. This was within a few months of the outbreak of World War I, but the argument was to be resumed after the war in relationship to the Bauhaus, and was carried on well into the 1950s. Even today the dispute is still relevant. Recently there has been a revival of interest in craftmanship and there is still a yearning for the objects of the craft shop which have been hand made and which in many cases are considered superior to some standardized machine made objects. As you will see from the extracts printed in *Documents*, the debate was partly about the status of the designer. Creativity and a measure of standardization were never considered incompatible. Now read the propositions and counter propositions and the speeches from the debate in *Documents*, 1.1–4. **How far can the points made in Muthesius's and Van de Velde's propositions be illustrated by the architecture and design in the 1914 exhibition?**

•   In considering the Muthesius–Van de Velde argument, it is important to realize that Van de Velde was not in favour of luxury articles, but was reacting against what he thought would devalue the position of the designer. He was old enough to have experienced some of the poor machine made articles of the nineteenth century, and to see the way manufacturers abused a design, and he feared a repetition of this. In 1897 he had made it quite clear that he was in favour of the widest possible market for his creations, using mass production (*Form and Function*, no. 8).

If you think back over the design situation from the mid-nineteenth century to 1914, it will be easy to see that the emphasis had always been on putting the art or soul into design. This is especially true of Vienna and Darmstadt before the founding of the DWB. It is therefore not surprising that designers, who a few years earlier had been encouraged to put the art back into design, reacted when they thought they were being told that individualistic genius was not relevant to the great universals of design. Muthesius was one of the few people at that time who was beginning to realize that the definition of designer, as it was in the early twentieth century, was unsuitable. The name designer at that time was really a pseudonym for 'artist who makes usable objects'. Muthesius said:

In any case art is far too pretentious a word for many sections of our activities, where it is simply a question of good taste, good decent forms and good proportions. So many catchwords have been engendered over the last ten years, such as 'art in the home', 'art in the street', 'shop-window art', 'student-living art' and 'art in a man's suit'—practically every word has to have 'art' tagged on—that the situation seems almost comic.

(H. Muthesius, 'The Task of the Werkbund in the Future' quoted in A305 D, *Documents*.)

In many ways, this viewpoint matches that of Adolf Loos (cf. *Form and Function*, nos. 20 and 21), who had ridiculed the Arts and Crafts aims of the Werkbund. Muthesius anticipated many of the repercussions of mass production, which the others, because they were basically artists, could not face. What Muthesius did not resolve was from what discipline this new designer should come. He realized that designers had to tackle problems in different ways to artists, but he did not know how to formulate this person or group of people. A new definition and category of designer was needed. In some ways he was too well grounded in the 'form follows function' theory to see the position of the designer clearly. What do you see as the inadequacies of the 'form follows function' idea? Think of furniture. Why do people design different sorts of tables and chairs, when the previous or already existing ones have been satisfactory to use? Were the DWB members any more justified in applying this catchword to their designs than Art Nouveau designers, many of whom believed that just a matter of using the fashionable Neoclassical and *Biedermeier* forms? ●

In these units we have discussed several different kinds of theory and stylistic manifestation. **Which of the following, on the evidence of the 1914 Cologne exhibition, were most pronounced just before the First World War?**

1   Arts and Crafts principles of craftsmanship, etc.
2   Vernacular revival
3   *Jugendstil*
4   Viennese Secession style
5   Massive, but simple, monumentality
6   Neoclassicism
7   The stripped rationalism of Behrens (as in the AEG factories)
8   The transparent symbolism of Gropius at the Fagus factory
9   Muthesius's stress on quality combined with industrial methods
10 Either Muthesius's concept of *type* (standardization), or Van de Velde's insistence on artistic independence (from the debate).

● This is intended as a revision exercise. You could use it when you are ready to work through the material again and sort out your ideas. In units like these, which cover a lot of ground, the final critical assessment and synthesis is particularly important if you are going to come away with a clear idea of the period. As we said at the beginning, it is not an easy episode to categorize in a few words, but the 1914 exhibition provides a useful test case to apply to all the ideas and developments of the previous decade or so. ●

Acknowledgements

Grateful acknowledgement is made to the following sources for material used in these units:

Figures

1 Architektonische Rundschau, 1897, plate 68; *2a and b, 3a–d* H. Muthesius, *Landhaus und Garten*, 1907, F. Bruckman Verlag; *4* BBC; *5a* Amsterdam Municipal Archives; *5b and 6* Max Eisler, *Kunst in Holland: Der baumeister Berlage*, Verlag Hölzel, Vienna; *7 and 8* Wurtembürgischer Landesmuseum; *9* H. Geretsegger and M. Peintner, *Otto Wagner 1841–1918*, 1964, Residenz Verlag; *10* Austrian National Library; *11 Der Architekt VII*, 1901; *12* Fr. Karla Hoffmann, *13–17* Olbrich Collection, Kunstbibliothek Stiftung Preussischer Kulturbesitz, Berlin. Photo: Paulmann; *18* B. Wilkins; *19 Pan* 1898 I; *21 and 22 Deutsche Kunst und Dekoration IX* 1901; *24* Bildarchiv Foto Marburg; *25 Deutsche Kunst und Dekoration XI*, 1902; *27–29 Studio Special Number*, 1906, 'Art Revival in Austria', Courtesy of Studio International; *32 and 33* Ludwig Münz and G. Künstler, *Der Architekt Adolf Loos*, 1964, Courtesy of Anton Schroll, Albertina, Vienna; *34 Chicago Tribune*; *35 Blatter für Architektur und Kunsthandwerk* 1888; *36 Dekorative Kunst* 1898/9; *37 Deutsche Konkurrenzen X*, 1899, Heft 3; *38 Deutsche Kunst und Dekoration XVII*, 1905/6; *39, 54 and 55* Kunsthistorisches Institut, Freie Universität, Berlin; *40, 41, 42 and 43* Franz Hoeber, *Peter Behrens*, 1913; *44 Kulturarbeiten, Dorfer und Kolonien III*, 1903; Photo: Stefan Muthesius; *45* Chevojon Frères, © S.P.A.D.E.M. Paris, 1974; *46* Dennis Sharp; *47* W. Muller-Wulckow *Bauten der Gemeinschaft aus Deutscher Gegenwart*, courtesy of Karl Robert Langewiesche Verlag; *48 Berlin und seine Bauten X*, courtesy of Verlag Wilhelm Ernst und Sohn; *50 and 51a and b* H. Weber, *Walter Gropius und das Fagusswerk*, 1961, courtesy of Verlag Georg D. W. Callweg, Munich; *52 and 53* photos: Tim Benton; *61* Allgemeine Elektrizitäts Gesellschaft; *62 Studio Yearbook*, 1910; *63 and 66 Deutscher Werkbund Jahrbuch* 1913; *64 Studio Yearbook* 1914; *65* Courtesy of Priscilla Roworth; *67–9* Münchner Stadtsmuseums; *70* Bruno Taut Archiv, Berlin, K. Junghanns *Brunno Taut 1880–1938*, 1970, Henschelverlag, Berlin.

Plates

1 H. Muthesius, *Kleinhaus und Kleinsiedlung* 1920, Munich; *2, 3, 23–26, 28–33, 36–38, 41–45, 47, 56–58, 63, 69, 81–83 and 85–93* photos: Tim Benton; *4–8, 17, 20 and 21* H. Muthesius, *Landhaus und Garten* 1907, F. Bruckman Verlag; *9, 10, 46, 71, 73–5, 77, 97, 110 and 112–13* Bildarchiv, Foto Marburg; *11, 76 and 99 Deutscher Werkbund Jahrbuch* 1912; *12* Copenhagen City Museum; *13 and 14* Kungl. Konsthögskolan School of Architecture, courtesy of Göran Lindahl; *15* J. Allan Cash; *16* Swedish Tourist Traffic Association. Photo: René Crispien; *18* BBC; *19* Museum of Finnish Architecture, Helsinki. Photo: H. Havas; *22* Museum of Finnish Architecture, Helsinki, Photo: N. E. Wickberg; *27, 34, 35 and 61* Austrian National Library; *39, 40 and 48* Hessisches Landesmuseum, Darmstadt; *49 and 50* Österreichisches Museum für Angewandte Kunst, Vienna. Photo: Ritter; *51* Franz Stoedtner; *52–3 and 55* Photos: Minders, Genk, *54* Photo: Ritter; *59–60 and 62* Loos-Archiv, Albertina, Vienna; *64 and 96* Karl-Ernst-Osthaus Museum, Hagen; *65* Kunstgeschichtliches Institut, Technische Hochschule, Munich. Photo: Gerhard Weiss; *66* H. Tessenow, *Hausbau und Bauten*, n.d.; *67* W. Muller-Wulckow, *Bauten der Gemeinschaft aus Deutscher Gegenwart*, 1928, Karl Robert Langewiesche; *68* Chevojon Frères © S.P.A.D.E.M., Paris, 1974; *70* Landesbildstelle, Berlin; *72 Deutsche Kunst und Dekoration XV*, 1904–5; *78–9* F. R. Yerbury, courtesy of Miss M. Morrison, Architectural Association; *80 and 84* AEG Telefunken; *94–5 Studio Yearbook* 1914. Photos: British Museum; *98* K. Huter, *Henry van der Velde* 1967, courtesy of Akademie Verlag; *100 and 101 Deutscher Werkbund Jahrbuch* 1914; *102 Studio Yearbook* 1910. Photo: British Museum; *103* Württembergisches Landesmuseum, Stuttgart; *104–9, 111 and 114–120 Deutscher Werkbund Jahrbuch* 1915.

Cover

Door of Wagner Villa II 1911–12. Photo: Tim Benton

History of architecture and design 1890–1939

Colour filmstrip illustrations associated with Units 5–6

1 Jugend *cover, June 1896 (Photo: BBC)*

2 Jugend *cover, April 1896 (Photo: BBC)*

3 *Otto Wagner, Majolika Haus, Vienna, 1898 (Courtesy Fratelli Fabbri Editori)*

4 *J. M. Olbrich, frieze design.* (Ideen von Olbrich, (*preface by L. Hevesi) Vienna, 1900.*)

5 *J. M. Olbrich, Ernst Ludwig Haus, Darmstadt, 1901 (Photo: Tim Benton)*

6 *Peter Behrens, drawing of the Behrens House, exhibited in the Darmstadt Exhibition, 1901* (Deutsche Kunst und Dekoraten, *vol IX 1901–2*)

7 *Peter Behrens, High Tension Factory on the AEG Brunnenstrasse site, Berlin, completed 1910 (Photo: Tim Benton)*

8 *Walter Gropius and Adolf Meyer, Fagus Shoe Last Factory, with the part of the Administration Building and the Machine Hall added 1913–4 (Photo: Tim Benton)*

9 *F. P. Glass, sample poster for 'Die Sechs', Munich, 1914 (München Stadtmuseum)*

10 *Ernst Naumann Studio, Berlin,* Manoli *advertisement* (Jahrbuch des Deutschen Werkbundes, *Berlin, 1913*)

11 *Joseph Hoffmann, design for linoleum* (Jahrbuch des Deutschen Werkbundes, *Berlin, 1913*)

12 *Peter Behrens, linoleum design for Anker Linoleum Company, Hamburg, c. 1913* (Jahrbuch des Deutschen Werkbundes, *Berlin 1913*)

1
2

1 *Richard Riemerschmid, houses in Hellerau garden city, near Dresden, c. 1910*   2 *Paul Schmitthenner, Staaken garden suburb, Berlin, 1914–1917*

5	
6	**8**
7	

5 *Hans Poelzig, own house, Breslau-Leerbeutel, 1904. Interior of staircase and hall* **6** *Hermann Muthesius, own house, Nikolassee, Berlin, 1906/7. Exterior* **7** *Dusan Jurkovic–Sebrowitz, wooden house in Resek, Bohemia, c. 1905. Exterior* **8** *Central living room-hall*

9 *Theodor Fischer, Erlöserkirche, Munich, 1899–1901* 10 *Theodor Fischer, Barracks church, Ulm, 1908–11. Exterior*
11 *Interior*

12 *Martin Nyrop, Town Hall, Copenhagen, designed 1888. Photo c. 1920* **13** *Ferdinand Boberg, Fire Station, Gävle, 1890*
14 *Detail* **15** *Ragnar Östberg, Stockholm City Hall, 1905–23. Exterior*

16	
17	**18**
19	

16 *Ragnar Östberg, Stockholm City Hall, 1905–23. Golden Hall. Interior* **17** *Ferdinand Boberg, own house,*
Stockholm, c. 1905 **18** *Ferdinand Boberg, Swedish Pavilion at the Universal Exhibition, Paris, 1900* **19** *Lars Sonck,*
Cathedral of Tampere, 1899–1901. Detail

20 *H. Gesellius, A. Lindgren and E. Saarinen, Hvitträsk, Kirkonummi, 1902. Exterior* **21** *Interior* **22** *Eliel Saarinen, Railway Station, Helsinki, 1904 (built 1909–14)*

31 *Otto Wagner, Flats at 4 Döblergasse, Vienna, 1910. Detail of main door* **32** *Otto Wagner, Flats at 40 Neustiftgasse, Vienna, 1912. Detail of corner* **33** *Otto Wagner, Wagner Villa II, Vienna, 1911–12 (designed 1905)* **33a** *Entrance*

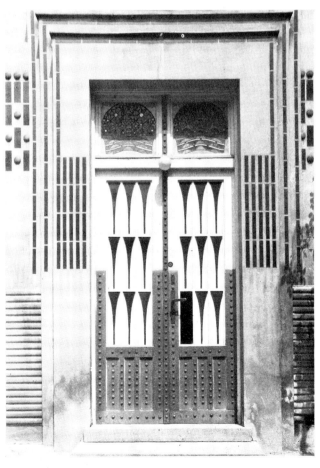

34 *J. M. Olbrich and Otto Wagner, Karlsplatz station for the Stadtbahn, Vienna, 1898–9* **35** *J. M. Olbrich, Secession building, Vienna, 1897–8*

36	
37	38

36 *Josef Hoffmann, Purkersdorf Sanatorium, near Vienna, 1903–6. Main front* **37** *Detail of entrance* **38** *View of garden front*

39	
	40
41	

39 *J. M. Olbrich, 2 silver candlesticks with amethysts (manufactured by P. Bruckmann and Sons, Heilbronn), 1901*
40 *J. M. Olbrich, Silver tea caddy with amethysts (manufactured by P. Bruckmann and Sons), 1901* **41** *Patriz Huber, Chair in cherrywood (made by the Glückert Hofmöbelfabrik), 1901*

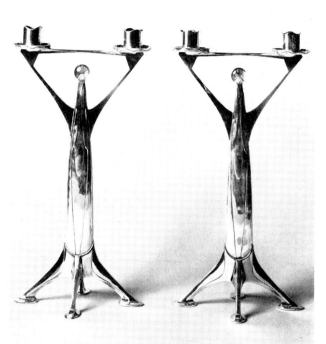

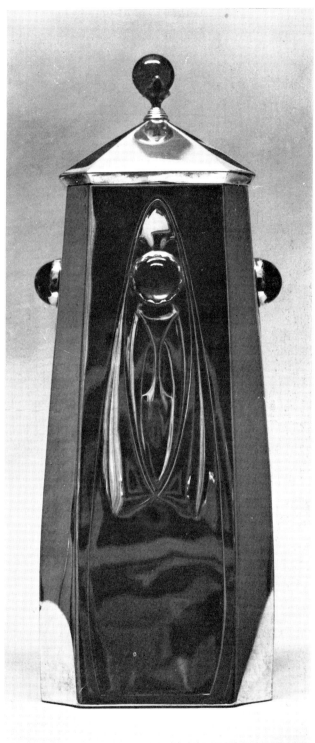

42 *J. M. Olbrich, Ernst Ludwig Haus, Darmstadt, 1900–01. Main entrance (statues by Ludwig Habich)*   43 *J. M. Olbrich, Glückert II house, 1901. Garden front*   44 *Entrance front*

45	47
	46

45 Hall   **46** J. M. Olbrich, *Hochzeitsturm (Wedding Tower), Matildenhöhe, Darmstadt, 1907–8*   **47** *Peter Behrens, own house in the artists' colony, Darmstadt, 1901*

69 *Anatole de Baudot, St. Jean de Montmartre, Paris, 1897–1900. Interior, detail of vaulting in aisle* **70** *Adolf Messel,*
Wertheim Department store. First part, begun 1897 **71** *Later section (1901)* **72** *Interior (1897)*

	69	
71	70	
	72	

73 | 74

75

73 *J. M. Olbrich, Tietz Department Store (now Kaufhof), Düsseldorf, 1906–8. Exterior* 74 *Interior* 75 *Hans Poelzig,*
Chemical Factory, Luban, 1911–12

76	77
78	79
	80

76 *Hans Poelzig, Water Tower, Posen, 1911. Interior showing exhibition area* **77** *Max Berg, Jahrhunderthalle, Breslau,* *1913. Exterior with part of the Breslau 1913 Exhibition buildings* **78** *Interior* **79** *Interior* **80** *Peter Behrens, AEG* *Turbine factory, Huttenstrasse, Berlin, 1908–9. Interior*

81	81a
82	83
	84

81 *Peter Behrens, AEG Turbine Factory, Huttenstrasse, Berlin, 1908–9* **82** *AEG Factory, Brunnenstrasse site: on the right, Johann Kraaz's Railway material building, 1904. In the centre, Behrens's first building for AEG, the Water Tower, 1907* **83** *Peter Behrens, High Tension factory 1910. West façade* **84** *Karl Bernhardt/Peter Behrens, preliminary sketch or High Tension factory, early 1909*

85 *Peter Behrens, Assembly Hall (north end) and, on left, new Railway material building, AEG, Brunnenstrasse site, Berlin, 1912–14* 86 *High Tension Factory, detail of main door on north flank* 87 *Walter Gropius and Adolf Meyer, Fagus Shoe Last factory, Alfeld-an-der-Leine, 1911–12. Corner of north-east and south-east side, from North East* 88 *Machine Hall on the south-west side, 1913–14*

89	
90	91 92
	93

Walter Gropius and Adolf Meyer, Fagus Shoe Last Factory, Alfeld-an-der-Leine: **89** *Power House and north corner of drying store, 1913–14* **90** *South-west front of Administration Building, 1913–14* **91** *North-west façade of drying store, 1911–14* **92** *Main entrance, 1913–14* **93** *Offices in the later part of the Administration Building*

104	105
106	107
	108
109	

DWB Exhibition, Cologne, 1914: **104** *Hermann Muthesius, Colour Pavilion* **105** *Peter Behrens, Main Hall* **106** *Josef Hoffmann, Austrian Pavilion* **107** *Walter Gropius and Adolf Meyer, Administration building of the model factory. Main front* **108** *Rear façade* **109** *Water Gropius and Adolf Meyer, Machine Hall*

110	
111	112
113	114

DWB Exhibition, Cologne, 1914: **110** *Henry Van de Velde, Theatre* **111** *Rear façade* **112** *Foyer* **113** *Interior*
114 *Bruno Taut, Glass Pavilion*

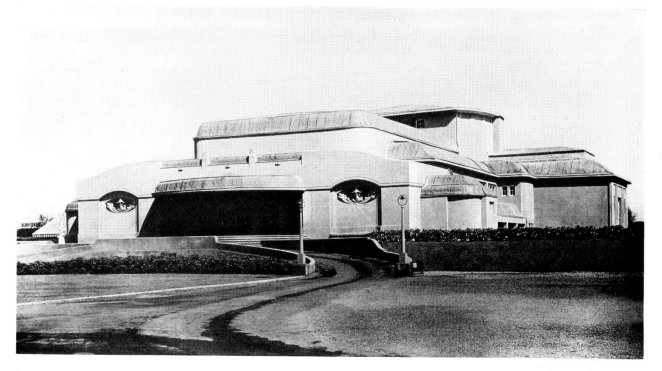

115 | 116
116 | 118
117 | 119
119 | 120

DWB Exhibition, Cologne, 1914: **115** *Josef Hoffmann, interior* **116** *H. Muthesius, Pavilion for the America-Hamburg shipping line. Interior* **117** *Behrens, Paul and Lonholdt, door handles* **118** *Henry Van de Velde, living room* **119** *Bruno Paul, study* **120** *Walter Gropius, Sideboard*

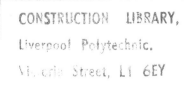